Ladies First~
SAINTS ALL

Philip B. Turner

Sponsored by:
History and Records Committee
of
The Bessie Gray Memorial United Methodist Church
P.O. Box 69
Caribou, Maine 04736

Distributed by Philip B. Turner
           P.O. Box 202
           Caribou, Maine
           04736

Book and Cover Design by GraphXperts Design Service – Woodstock, NB
Cover Painting by niece Suzzanne Noe

Printed in Canada

ISBN 1-896775-20-9

Turner, Philp B., 1922 –

— Dedication —

This Book is dedicated to
Bessie Gray,
a remarkable Methodist Lady.

— Acknowledgement —

As is our custom, wife Jean reads and offers her thoughts.
This book would not be the same without her help.

Bessie's Father & Mother

Bessie & Sister

— Introduction —

The need for this book was made known to the author when he returned from visiting relatives in the Carolinas. There before his eyes was a banner showing the church building with James Gray's picture but not Bessie's. It is time to tell everyone that the church on the corner of Sweden and Prospect in Caribou, Maine, is officially The Bessie Gray Memorial United Methodist Church.

After serious consideration I decided that the best way to present this history was to have Bessie write a diary in which I have used the facts available. When one is sixteen life may be –"What shall I do?" Bessie knew and she recorded it in her diary.

Bessie did make mistakes in writing, a few I left, many I corrected. Sometimes her pencil was so dull it left only poor marks. Her pen was more legible. She did her best.

Then I asked, "Were there more Bessies in the Methodist past?"

After quizzing fifty United Methodist Bishops I found – yes there were. And so I have added these names at the end of the book. Most, like Bessie, were GOD'S SAINTS.

All facts that were available were used.
Fiction was used to make the story.

Ladies First~
Saints All

Philip B. Turner

Stella Hodgdon

Bob Hodgdon

Diary

1889-1894

Annie McPhee

Leo McPhee

*My First writing in my New Blue Diary
by Bessie Beatrice Raworth in Port Elgin,
County of Westmoreland, New Brunswick, Canada.*

March 31, 1889

> *Every day the Ra
> in my name
> rhymes with hay
> say it Rayworth*

March 31, 1889 – My Birthday

We had all gone to the old Presbyters church – it is
better than having classes at peoples' homes – this
Sunday – as we always do – even in a rain storm – and as
soon as we got home – and I took off my wet clothes, and
Papa gave me this new blue diary on my sixteenth
birthday. It's got a blue leather cover and dates on the
pages for the next five years. I wonder what my last
entries will be? We had a nice Sunday dinner. Grandpa
Raworth and Grammy spent the afternoon with us. Reta
and me did the dishes and then Ernest filled the wood
boxes and helped Papa do the barn chores. Courtney,
who is a man now, left to see his latest girlfriend,
Elderina.

Before I went to bed upstairs, I thanked Papa and gave
him a kiss. Papa said, Now Bessie, you do know how to
read and write so you keep a good diary starting today. I
am in grade 10. Mum came up the stairs and whispered
in my ear that she had a little money and that we would
go and buy me a new dress as soon as she could find the

time. I hope it is blue. I have blue eyes and some say they are pretty. Then I wrote this by candle while the wind blew down from the north and howled and tried to sneak in any small crack. After our prayers we will crawl under the pile of blankets and hope to soon fall asleep.

May 5, 1889

It is spring, the sun is shining, and we had a young, so good looking man – he is a tailor – James Gray – in the pulpit today. I tried to get Papa to invite him to have Sunday dinner with us. But no. Papa can be stubborn and when his ice blue eyes say no, I know enough to be still. He just invited Grandpa and Grammy like always.

I'll be an old maid – a dried up old prune, if Papa keeps guarding the door. He is James Gray and he has a very nice face. I think he is planning on going to Mount Allison college, but right now he is one of the tailors in town. Sister tried to tease me, but I pushed her off, but we did spend a long time after our prayers talking about boys in general. I am not going to college – that's for men but I'm not going to live the life of a spinster either. Ever since I became a Christian and had my sins washed away, I had thought and dreamed that if God wanted me to go to some place like the wilds of Africa then I would do all that I could to be ready. So I'm going to help in every way I can at the church and study my Bible every living day. I have been taking organ lessons from our Church organist, Miss Blanche Turner. She is Botsford's daughter, she will soon be playing in our own new church building. They laid the cornerstone in '88 after Hazen Copp donated the land. I'll be ready to help win souls for Christ.

May 19, 1889

Papa did it! He had to have a new suit of Sunday clothes so Papa went to the local tailor shop and James is now sewing him a new suit. He invited James to have Sunday dinner and Grandpa and Grammy begged off to go on a picnic with some other very old people. Papa must have heard my prayers, for the door was opened and James walked into my heart. He doesn't know it yet but I'm sure God has picked me out to be James' helper. I'll go with him even if he doesn't go to Africa. Yes, I think I'll be his helpmate just like it says in the Bible and it also says go forth and multiply.

I am not letting my sister nor anyone else read this, for Reta is too young to think those thoughts. I did my best in all my conversations with James to let him know that I was truly a Christian ready to do God's work in this His world. I was glad Grandpa was not at the table today for he does make a mess of his waist coat when he spoons the chicken soup past his white beard. Grammy says she is gonna cut it off some night when Grandpa is snoring in their bed. She never will. I hope James never grows a beard that large to dip into the soup I might serve him in Africa. I wonder what kind of soup they make in Africa? We have chicken most every Sunday. I'll let God decide.

June 2, 1889

James took part with Rev. Teed in the service today at the Methodist service in the old Presbyter church. I have been teaching Sunday school for the very young children. James did not have Sunday dinner with us today. The Rev. Teed wanted to talk with him so he ate there.

June 15, 1889

I went to Milton's store to buy a few things for Mum and I met my good old friend Elda Murray. We have been the best of friends since we first went to school. I just had to tell her about my crush on James. And she said he was the most handsome man in town and I deserved to get him. I told her about my dreams at night and my dreams of day which have all fallen on my James, dear James. I see him in the morning shaving. I see him eating his breakfast. I see him with his arms around me. I dream his lips on mine. I dream of James.

June 26, 1889

I met some of the tailors living at Fred Clarks when I stopped to speak with James last evening. Calis Matheson, Lorenza Howard, and William MacLeod. They were polite. They know Courtney as he has just started a small woodworking business. Father is going to help him with some money. My brother is very smart in business.

June 28, 1889

Our town Port Elgin has been called Gaspareau, I think that is a fish name, and it was called the Bridge and sometimes the Bend. But we call it Port Elgin now in honor of Thomas Bruce, the 7th Earl Elgin. School is out next week and I am going to help mother plant our garden. We will plant a few flowers.

Father has planted oats, buckwheat, potatoes and a few rows of corn.

Nov. 2, 1890

My dear James came home to preach at our church here in Port Elgin as a **Licensed** preacher. Papa invited him for Sunday Dinner. I greeted him at the door with a kiss on his entrance. Never mind that all the family was there watching. Dear James is now going to apply to that school in Boston. A real theological school they say. He is going to finish up his studies at Mount Allison Academy this winter in Sackville over in N.B.

So we went on a good long walk after we had finished eating. James said we might be able to get married as soon as he finished at Mount Allison. He feels sure he can find a church that can pay enough for us to live on. He is quite conservative on money and has saved money while being a tailor. After he goes back to Mount Allison he promised and I promised to write. We stopped and had a drink of Papa's apple cider, then I walked him home. We kissed most every time that we could without an audience. I was all in a heat by the time he left me and he entered his boarding house. I'll miss him – my dear, dear James. I'll dream that dream again and again. We are getting married. I am going to be Mrs. Gray, the preacher's wife.

Dec. 20, 1890

James came home yesterday. He will have the evening service at our new Methodist church building. I will give my testimony and play the organ. We will have time to take a sleigh ride to some friends in Tidnish Bridge, we might stay overnight if they ask.

Dec. 23, 1890

On our sleigh ride James told me about his classmates at the Academy. He said David Allen was a good student and always helped the Newfie, Indox. He had had little schooling. James Smith, Asa Strong and Jim Wheatly did quite well. I asked James how he did and he said he was the top student. Dr. Harrison was the Principal and Albert Mack was their music teacher. James said they were good Methodist men and teachers.

Dec. 25, 1890

James gave me a ring and many kisses last night. We did stay overnight with Jack Freeze and his wife Dolly. Jack has a large farm with many cows, sheep and other animals. It had snowed a lot on our trip here and they said that driving back in our pung was not the safe thing to do. It would be easy to lose the road and get lost in the dark. It snowed some all night. When we left our friends we said now you will come to our wedding. They said they would come but they would have to come back on the railroad (they said, cars) after the wedding to tend the animals. That's farming for you. No days off.

James' brother has invited me to supper. They were both born in New Castle-on-Tyne, England. James' father, John, was born in Scotland and his mother, Rachel, in Ireland.

Feb. 20, 1891

Now that James and I are engaged I can write him my deepest thoughts. And he has written me his. I know now that we were meant to be together for we both long to do God's work. I will help him bring many souls to know Jesus no matter where we are called. *"In all thy ways acknowledge Him and He shall direct thy paths" Proverbs*

We have had a lot of rain for this month and the fishermen are having a hard time with their boats as the rain turns to ice and they spend most of the working days chipping it off.

I am glad my father and brothers do not fish for a living.

May 1, 1891

The letter came and James says we will be married soon.He has found a church in Amherst, Nova Scotia that can pay him enough so we can live while he – no us – we – wait for a yes from that college in Boston. Father says he will make us a bed, he is a good carpenter. Mother said that I had better think about some household things. I will find some work as soon as school is over. I have one more year at Superior. I learned that my teachers in the first few years of school spelled my name with a "y". Rayworth. I am going to make sure that when I finish Superior school that it is as Bessie Raworth.

Aug. 3, 1891

I went on a picnic with some of the friends that I had in school, Tammy Copp, Davis Allen, Royal Anderson and Sam Turner were some of the boys. Of course Elda Murray came and Cilia Simpson, Eva Robinson, cousin Cora Silliker, and yes, George Lamoreaux. William

Chapman and Charles Murray had gone out on a fishing boat. I was glad because Charles always wants to kiss me. I am in love with James now and Charles is just an old friend. No more. We all had a great time together eating and singing.

July 6, 1892

I am going to be **married** this afternoon in a brand new lovely **BLUE** dress. My dear, dear James came from Amherst and has been here in Port Elgin since Saturday. Papa and Mum sent out the invites. We will be married in our new Methodist church. Courtney and Elda (Elderina Murray) will stand up with us. Rev. Johnson has come over from Baie Verte. Then we are going to go over to the Island for a few days. I have to get ready now. More later.

July 14, 1892

Back from Prince Edward Island and now at Port Elgin. Going and coming the sea was rough and waves dashed against the boat but I did not get sick. My dear, so dear, husband is very kind and gentle. We both were as green as grass yet we found ourselves loving and loving.

July 15, 1892

James reads from the Bible every morning and then we have a time of worship. We started doing this on the morning after our wedding. It makes us closer to our maker and to each other.

Aug. 2, 1892

We stayed here in Port Elgin because Rev. Johnson asked James to stay for the dedication of our finished and paid for church. There were lots of things to do and we both did our best to help the great day be a memorable one.

Rev. Johnson was the district Superintendent at the time we decided to build a new church building and had been one of the ministers to recommend James for his Licensing. We had Rev. Teed, Rev. Chapman, Rev. McKay here for the dedication. A very large choir led by Mrs. Clark, my piano teacher, Miss Blanche Turner, on the organ and the Port Elgin Band led by Mr. Dakin. Much credit was given to Mr. Hazen Copp for his land and his money and the gift of the organ. Too bad he was already buried in the cemetery.

My Aunt Susannah Monro (Raworth) came to my wedding and she also came to the church dedication. Mother said she was house-bound after the wedding. She looked quite well today. I went over and gave her a hug and a kiss.

Sept. 20, 1892

We came over on the cars and soon was at Amherst, Nova Scotia. James is going to preach in the Methodist church on Amherst Point on Sunday the 24 and I will be there in my new BLUE Sunday-go-to-meeting dress, my marriage dress that I took with us to Prince Edward Island. Now I and dear James will do the Lord's work here in Amherst. I am ready to give my testimonial about how I accepted Jesus as my Savior. I like to tell that story for it makes me feel warm all over to know that I am going to be with HIM, my Jesus. I am so proud of my dear husband's first sermon here. He practiced it last night and it was very well done. Better than some of the older men. He is a great persuader for his voice sounds like the truth.

I am not a trained musician but I can play the piano and organ – passably and my voice is pleasant. So I told my dear James that I would do whatever needed to be done in any of his churches.

Aug. 10, 1892

It is twelve miles from Amherst to the Point. James bought a very good horse and wagon for this Sunday trip. I will go with him Sundays and Wednesdays when they have prayer meetings. I am glad we are going to stay here in Amherst. The Point has one store and the small church. Most of the members are farmers. A few own boats and fish. I am sure they will give us some fish once in awhile. I have started a Sunday school with twelve girls and six boys.

Oct. 24, 1892

The newspapers here are spending too much time telling us what is going on in the States. Most people here don't know what a Democrat or a Republican stand for. I surely don't. But the papers make Cleveland and Harrison sound like dim-wits. One will be the President of the United States. There are two others running for that office, I'll have to get the paper to write their names – Weaver and Bidwell. They are not names we have heard of before. Our Macdonald has been doing the right thing in Ottawa, keep the American and British at bay and let Canada tend to her trading on her terms. Not to be another state for the U.S.A. When I vote I'll vote for Macdonald's party.

Amherst is quite a large town and we have found that there are a lot of things you can buy here that you never found in Port Elgin. Fruits of many kinds and quite cheap. Pineapple and Bananas.

Dec. 4, 1892

We have a large Sunday School and I have the teenage boys and girls. They are a nice and well-behaved group. I am going to have 2 or 3 of them every night for supper so they can get to know us better. James said if the children come to church, soon the parents will follow.

Dec. 28, 1892

We had a Christmas play at the church. My teenage group put it on and it filled the church with adults. James took a collection and it was a most generous one. The Trustees will have enough money to start putting electric lights in the church this coming spring.

Cleveland won in the U.S.A.

Jan. 30, 1893

James keeps writing to that college in Boston and they keep asking for this and that. Letters have been sent to them from about everyone who knows my dear James. And yet they ask for more. He has his heart fixed on that Boston school of Theology and he is determined that they will accept him soon.

May 5, 1893

I have gone to the third doctor at my dear mother's asking. I think that it just might be that the Lord has made me barren so that I can spend all my awake hours helping my James do the Lord's work.

Aug. 20, 1893

Word that at this time they did not have an opening for my James at that college in Boston. I like it here in Amherst and we are winning many souls for CHRIST.

The Methodist members at the Point gave James a small raise in pay and we are doing quite well. I have found a lot of good friends here in Amherst and the Point.

Dec. 25, 1893

Christmas and we had invited Jack and Molly Freeze to come have Christmas with us but their many animals kept them home. When we go next to Port Elgin we will stop to see them. My sister, Reta did come over last Sept. for a few days visit. I have asked Father and Mother, but

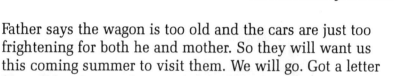

Father says the wagon is too old and the cars are just too frightening for both he and mother. So they will want us this coming summer to visit them. We will go. Got a letter from Elda Murray, she says her brother Charles married Cilia Simpson and that she and (the always late) Lamoreaux are planning on a wedding in the spring. I bet he will be late at their wedding – she should plan on it.

Jan. 5, 1894

A pair of horses ran away yesterday and they pulled the wagon over a man and killed him. He was John Freeland, a member of our church. He had a wife and five little children. Fran, the oldest is one of my girls. The wife will likely sell the farm and come to town. James will have to do his first funeral. I will play the piano for the service.

Jan. 10, 1894

The District Superintendent came and had an evening meal with us. He told James that the church members at the Point hope he will stay with them for some time. He said he liked what we have done at the Point.

March 30, 1894

Last page in First diary. February was rain and snow and it all turned to ice.

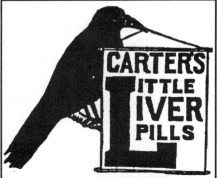

Diary

1894 – 1899

April 1, 1894

I bought a new five-year diary. It is the same size as the one father bought me but it is deeper blue. The printing on the cover looks like gold leaf. It cost me 38 cents. I bet that's more than Father paid. I hope this one records James and I going to Boston. I will ask for my God's help in that matter.

April 3, 1894

The sun came out and melted all of the ice. Now the street needs to be cleaned for the horse manure is thick and if it lies there and dries it will blow into the houses and stink.

April 10, 1894

They did not clean up the manure but it rained and the water poured down the hills and now every valley is a manure pile. Maybe some farmer will collect it. We never had this problem at the Port for most people lived on farms.

May 12, 1894

Some people did collect the manure. I would have if we had room for a garden. Helping James is a full-time job and I am happy doing it. We are in God's service. They are nearly finished with the electric lights in the church. No word from Boston but James says he prays about it and the Lord has told him to wait and not to lose HOPE. James is sure he will be going to that school.

April 4, 1895

We went home. Grampy Raworth died and James was asked to do the funeral. The people came from all around and James gave a very good sermon. That night after the men had gone to bed Mother asked why I had not gotten with child. Well, I have thought that maybe I should see another doctor. I again promised mother I would when I got back to Amherst. She said Cousin Jamie had got that way and now was trying to persuade her man to marry her. Well I wanted to become pregnant and Jamie probably did not want to.

May 3, 1895

A new prime minister every other day. But really do we need to keep changing the head of Canada government?? They all seem to say the same thing.

Aug. 22, 1895

Well we made it and was father and mother happy to see us in Port Elgin and James will have the service Sunday. We slept at my home. The bed squeaks but my parents are both quite hard of hearing. You must look them right in the face to make them understand you. Courtney took us to see his woodworking factory. And my it is big and he has over twenty men doing sawing and spooling. Father was a carpenter but my Courtney makes many things from wood for sale. I did get to see some of my schoolmates at the store.

Aug. 30, 1895

We will go back to Amherst at noon tomorrow on the railroad. Mother asked me again why I wasn't pregnant. I said I'd see another doctor in Amherst.

Sept. 10, 1895

I have made a trip to see another doctor. Dr. Rallis said I should keep track of my monthly and bring it to him after six months. Now I hope he can give me the good news as how a child is to be born to us. Mother told me again about a cousin who did not have a child for several years and then they came every other year. Maybe I'll do the same. James says a boy or girl will suit him. He has names for both when they come, and I have prayed and will call on the Lord for this event to come soon.

Dec. 26, 1895

We had the largest congregation this Christmas Sunday that they ever had at the Point Church. We both thank God for the many souls we are bringing to Christ, and for them a new way to live. No letter from the College in Boston this year.

Dec. 29, 1895

A telegram came to tell us that Uncle Jacob Raworth had gone to meet his maker. They will have his funeral service at the church.

July 1, 1896

We got a telegram. My Uncle William's wife Ruth passed away in her sleep and father wants James to come do the funeral service.

July 3, 1896

We arrived – covered with coal dust and hungry – at Port Elgin and my father and mother were happy to see us with kisses. After we had eaten and taken a bath we crawled into my old bed and soon dropped off to a sound sleep.

July 4, 1896

James will lead the service Sunday. James had the funeral at two in the afternoon. Aunt Barbara and Uncle James Dobson came. Uncle Joe Dobson came alone. His wife was away visiting their son in Saint John. Not many other relatives came – some are too feeble to make the trip to the church. Another good night's rest in my old bedroom – the springs squeak but we ignored them.

July 5, 1896

It is Sunday and we all go to church. James was very powerful, and I told of my commitment to the Lord Jesus. All my relations were there even that one who had a baby and no marriage. Father was especially pleasant to her. Seems that most families have this problem. Father would have been devastated if it had happened with his children.

July 8, 1896

We will go back to Amherst at six tomorrow on the train. Mother asked me again why I wasn't pregnant. I said I had seen a doctor in Amherst.

Aug. 4, 1896

I have made a trip to see ANOTHER doctor. They all say the same thing but it does not work...

Aug. 8, 1896

What a downpour we had with lightning crashing all night long. James, dear James, had very little sleep. The new horse was scared and made a lot of noise and James went to the stable to comfort her. This young mare has only been away from her mother a few months and I think she misses her.

Aug. 10, 1896

We had the second wedding in the family and what a lot of relatives came to the marriage of Courtney and Eldora Murray. We spent a week at home in the Port.

Aug. 30, 1896

James, even without proper sleep, delivered a very warming sermon. Many came to the front to renew or to declare their allegiance to Jesus. That husband of mine can sway people for the good of God's Kingdom.

Sept. 2, 1896

That young mare, Dolly, upset James in the wagon when a train blew its whistle down in the lower part of town when he was going to the Point. I thank God he was not hurt, but the wagon will need quite a lot of repair. I can pass on that new winter coat, I know a lady that can do the needed mending. AT LONG LAST A LETTER from that college in Boston saying that James can come in the fall of 1897.

James is delighted but I must say that if my James had not been so persistent he never would have been accepted. What a long drawn-out ordeal. So many letters sent from James' many friends and so many not now but later letters from Boston. Now – I hope that the Lord favors us in Boston – for my dear James sake.

Jan. 1, 1897

This is the year that we will leave and go to Boston. James has a great Uncle there and will write him soon.

Feb. 4, 1897

Mother sent me a long letter with lots of news about the Port. Many of my school mates and cousins have moved away. Courtney is making money and the woolen mill is doing well. One of father's sisters, Sarah, has died and left father a small property.

Feb. 20, 1897

A letter from mother saying that my rich older brother, Courtney, has a big bouncy boy named Rupert. She said he looked like the Murrays.

March 3, 1897

We got a letter from Boston from James' Uncle Gray. He said he could take us in for a few months until we found our own place to rent.

March 10, 1897

I have missed my period. I have not ever done that. I will tell James but not just yet. I am praying that I am **pregnant.**

April 7, 1897

I told James and we both hugged and cried and laughed. James said, he would like a boy and a girl – why not twins? James says we will call them John and Rachel to memorialize his parents both have died just a few years ago in Prince Edward Island.

May 5, 1897

I thought about sending a telegram to Mother. But a voice inside said good news will keep. If the Lord is willing I can send her a birth message from Boston.

June 4, 1897

Monday we sold the mare, Dolly, and the wagon for a nice price. We sold all our meager furniture rather than pay to have it shipped to Boston. Had a going away supper with all our friends and parishioners at the church. I have found many friends in Amherst and the Point. We have laughed and prayed over good times and sad times. I have told a few of those good friends that I was expecting.

June 6, 1897

My dear James got us on the stage to Amherst Point. We are going to take a coaster to Boston. It will be my first long trip on the ocean.

The Boston Theology school wrote James to come. The school said they would send a few students to meet us and help us to Hyde Park to Uncle Thomas Gray's place. Dear James says it is not too far from the school and that I will like it better than living in Boston.

June 8, 1897

My, the waves are big and the ship rocks side to side as we leave the Minas Basin. We had a good night's sleep last night but if this continues I'm going to be sick. I **am** sick. I cannot hold the pen!

June 9, 1897

The rain came down and the wind blew all night and I did not sleep. I have had a few pains in my stomach. I think it is the food. It is much different than what we normally eat.

June 12, 1897

Yesterday in the night **I lost** my baby. I did pain some and thought it was all that strange food. The ship's doctor came and took it away. James said it was a boy and he was so small you could have laid his head on your index finger and his feet would have just touched your wrist.

June 13, 1897

I left the cabin but the wind has come searching for us from all directions. The waves break over the bow and I am afraid. I don't swim and where would we swim to? I came back and crawled onto the bed. James brought me something to eat – which I could not keep down!

June 14, 1897

James was only slightly sick and now he seems to rather enjoy this ride. I will never take another ship. NEVER – NEVER! James brings me my food. I have prayed that I will be able to have another baby soon. I am still bleeding some. Our sheets were wet every morning.

June 16, 1897

I can't do much writing – the ship rolls and plunges and I will never take a boat again.

June 18, 1897

Finally we are entering the Boston Harbor and for the last two days my stomach has stopped flipping and turning. Yet the sheets are wet with my blood in the mornings. I will be glad to put my feet on solid ground. James has our things ready to go. The school said they would send someone to meet us at the dock. I hope we are on schedule and that I and dear James can find a nice little place to stay in Hyde Park after our stay with Uncle.

June 19, 1897

Well, we were met by two young students, Frederick Griffith who said he lived in Hyde Park and Gordon Ross who came from Port Greenhill, N.S. We were both glad for this city is large and very strange. They were most helpful in getting our things onto the cars that took us out to Hyde Park and then we stopped at an eatery where I rested and the three men went looking for the right cars to take to Hyde Park Ave. James' Uncle Thomas Gray lives at 221. He has been in America for several years and has a shoddy mill. We finally got there and Uncle lives in a house that has two back bedrooms – you go up back stairs. His dear wife, Mary came and helped us settle our few things in the back bedroom. It had a bed and a lampstand. The front room had a table and a few chairs. The Grays are about fifty and invited us to have our first meal with them. Mary said I could use her kitchen for cooking.

June 27, 1897

James took some of our savings so he could buy some needed things for our home in America. We both thanked our God every night on that most hazardous trip over His sea. But I'll not trespass on it again. From what I saw as we entered the city and left I will not venture alone into that hubbub place. There are just too many freight wagons and fancy coaches and cabs and they all seem to be going so fast and with complete disarray. I am glad to be in the small village of Hyde Park even if it is strange in many ways. There are metal working plants also chemical and many woolen mills.

July 1, 1897

James is going to do some tailoring for one of the clothing stores here in Hyde Park. Mr. Henry Routley has an opening for James to do the extra work at his shop which is just opposite the Masonic Temple. It will be just for the unexpected that comes along. James said a few more dollars will let his wife gain some of the weight that she lost coming to America. There is a great big Methodist Church on Central Avenue and the corner of Winthrop Street here in Hyde Park. It is near the telephone company building. We are going to be members. The Pastor is Frank T. Pomeroy. He is a very large man and has a wife.

July 4, 1897

We had an outing – to escape the hot summer! James had a small job at the clothing store. We went to Plymouth to see where the Puritans landed. We took our lunch. We rode the train and trolleys. Fred Griffith and Gordon Ross went with us. The rock is not much to see, but it was fun to do something different.

July 6, 1897

There was a lot of talk in the neighborhood about Uncle Gray's fire at the shoddy mill. One of his dryers caught fire. The firemen did a great job of putting it out before it had burned too much of the building.

Aug. 3, 1897

The market had a lot of cheap fruit and we are eating it in breads and pies. We have gone visiting for new

Methodists to join our Sunday school class. Rev. Pomeroy had asked James to be the teacher. NOW we will visit those that have not yet committed to our Lord Jesus Christ and ask them to join the Methodist church here in Hyde Park.

Aug. 15, 1897

Our small Sunday school, that meets at the Methodist Church, of our neighbor families of new Irish people has grown to twenty. We have asked them to invite their friends to the Methodist Sunday morning worship.

Aug. 23, 1897

We have found a nice rent with a kitchen and a large bedroom. Not too far from the New Haven Railroad Station. Most people in this part of Hyde Park are Irish or Scotch. Now! I needed that privacy for I am still bleeding. James has made me promise to see a doctor. We met with the new families that came last Sunday. The McKennas, Whites and Jones. The Sunday School Superintendent asked us to make a special effort to greet and get to know any new people that came to the Sunday service.

Sept. 1, 1897

My James says that he is going to start going to Boston College of Theology soon. He will go in town today. WE Praise God! Both the McKennas and the Jones families were baptized Sunday. The Whites are going to at Christmas, when their parents might come.

James had to buy his first shoes in America and they were very costly, $2.59. He got them at Haskels Shoe shop. It was about a week's worth of work at the tailor shop.

Sept. 10, 1897

BOSTON

The hot summer is over and James is now going off to school in Boston. He takes the cars every morning. Now I have the whole day to buy the food. The fish is just as good as home, but they have more vegetables in the store. I visit with a young mother on the floor below us. Annie McPhee has two children. Her husband, Leo, works at the metal stamping factory. I like to visit with her. She came here from Ireland with her husband. When I found that out I asked her how she liked the trip over in the boat. That was when I told her about my resolve never to go on the sea again. She was carrying her first child, Harry, and was sick all the way over. I did go see a Doctor in Hyde Park – a Dr. K. McHight, he was most careful in his exam. He told me that I would never get pregnant again. And he said he could not promise that he could stop the blood from flowing. I am still praying that it will happen. I remember that my Christ stopped the flow of a woman's blood. It was her faith, He said.

Sept. 17, 1897

I read the Sunday newspaper on Monday sometimes. That President William McKinley, a Republican, is pushing for higher tariffs and against silver. I have not read a Canadian newspaper since we left Amherst. The American papers say very little about Canada. It is mostly about Spain, Cuba, and some place called Philippines. Some Americans are fighting. Roosevelt is in the paper every time I read it. I posted James' letter to his brother, Sam. James is asking if he would like to come to Boston to be a tailor. The pay for that is a lot more here than they pay at Port Elgin.

Oct. 10, 1897

A few weeks ago the District Superintendent came to our Sunday school class and asked us if we would start a Methodist class for some of the unchurched people in Hyde Park. Now we have a class of ten – eight women and two men. Both the men work at American Tool and Machinery here in Hyde Park. We are going to tell them about the New Testament. James is reading and then explaining it to them. A letter from Mum, they are all well but she asked again if there was any grandchild on the way. I think MOTHER has a one track mind on this – now I will write and tell her that she has lost a grandson. I am still devastated. That only baby of mine never had a Christian burial. James said, that they buried him like all those that die at sea. I am glad I was so sick that I did not see them toss him in the – the raging ocean.

October 14, 1897

Edgar Jones, who came to study at the school, is from Newfoundland, we call them Newfies. He helped us in the Sunday School services and stayed for Sunday dinner. He liked my apple pie. He ate nearly half of it. James is doing well in school and at the store. I have been helping the young ladies form a sewing class. First we study the Bible and then learn how to sew. Fred Griffith, Edgar and James are planning a revival meeting for here in Hyde Park. They are so enthused about it and the people of the Sunday School classes are too. They plan it for some week of November.

Oct. 15, 1897

Today I went with James to Boston. I rode on the train. It goes so fast I was dizzy. And then when we got off there was a mighty lot of horses – some going fast, others pulling large wagons loaded with something. And a few automobiles all racing head-long down the street and blowing their horns. I didn't think it was safe to cross the street but we did, and then I was escorted to the University library. James then went off to class. The newspapers say that they are building a tunnel under the city and that trains will carry people in that hole. I will beg off from that adventure. I should say that the Library was just magnificent and I read a lot of magazines that I had never seen at all ever. Some from Canada!

Oct. 22, 1897

The Sunday newspaper is full of trouble with Spain, Cuba, and Hawaii and it seems that they, the Spaniards, do not treat the natives very fairly. Got a letter today from my folks. Mother is well and misses us. She did say that she was most sorry for our loss and that she knew of some women who had children after they had lost the first one. Father and Ernest, who is 18 now, are working hard to get the work done before it becomes too cold. Sister Reta is 15 now and is still in school. Ernest is finished now and may go into the wood works to help Courtney who has a big mill in Port Elgin. It is very nice weather here in Hyde Park. It was very hot this summer. This October weather is more to my liking.

Oct. 29, 1897

I have been quite sick this week and James sent me to a doctor. He gave me some pills to try. As I was leaving I got my courage up and asked the doctor if he could tell me why I did not get pregnant and if my flow of blood would ever cease. He then asked me so many questions that at the end of it, I wish I had not asked. And then he told me so many possible reasons that I let them all in one ear and out the other. He gave me some pills for iron which he thought might pep me up. I am now of the opinion that I must be barren so that I can do more of God's work.

Nov. 3, 1897

The Jones have twins. That makes them four young children. Helen wants a larger place to live but her husband says she will have to do with the one she lives in. He also said, "More kids and more food will eat up that last dollar raise" he got for doing a good job at the Scott woolen mill. He cards there.

Nov. 15, 1897

Today I walked around the neighborhood on the other side of the rail tracks and visited with many Irish women. I found that many have no church and are without knowledge of the saving grace of Jesus. When James gets back from school I'll have supper ready and I will tell him about these women. Should we not start a Methodist class in that part of town soon? We could have them here in our place. We need to do God's work here in Hyde Park. Now that walk did help my pain and so I will visit all people in Hyde Park with God's help.

Nov. 23, 1897

The big rally was held last night. We had it at the Methodist church dining hall. For the sing after the meal we went up to the sanctuary. It has a pipe organ and I enjoyed playing it very much. We had a very good crowd and many came and repented of their sins. John Terry, The Pastor Rev. Whitaker, David Bancroft, George Stocking, trustees came and helped us.

A letter from Sam telling us that he had finally had a calling to be an evangelist and has started down that path. He said that Courtney had expanded his wood-working mill and now had over 50 men working for him. The woolen mill was still doing quite well and fishing had been good all year. Cod and Lobsters.

Dec. 2, 1897

James had a really great meeting at the M.E. church dining hall for both of our study groups. They are called EPWORTH LEAGUE. We organized them in this one group. Elected to be President was Geo. Dotty, Miss Helen Chamberlain was chosen as Vice-President.

Dec. 13, 1897

We had some snow last night. I will just go visiting today in the area next to where we live. I keep tabs on the new families that move in. James says it helps to be there to greet them first. I find that I can help them much more now that I have the experience. My, they all seem to have more children than we did in Port Elgin. But I remain barren. The iron pills did give me more energy.

Dec. 20, 1897

Plans are under way to have a big Christmas party in the M.E. Church dining hall. With all our Sunday School members – with the almost committed Christians that we now have and the ones that have been asked by us and the minister to attend we will have nearly sixty.

Dec. 31, 1897

All that work and still when this year is over we will have only 20 new confirmed members for our First Methodist Episcopal Church here in Hyde Park.

Jan. 1, 1898

HYDE PARK
We had sixty-two at our Christmas service. Marcus Buell, the Dean and Professor of New Testament, came and helped with the singing. He has a very pleasant voice which caused all the congregation to sing loud and I played the pipe organ up right smartly.

Feb. 3, 1898

A letter from home. Mother says they are well and the boys are doing fine. She asked if I were in a family way. How I wish I could send her word that I was. The work that I do bringing these unchurched men and women to know Christ will have to be my work and not a family. Dear James has stopped asking and I have asked the doctors but they are of no help. Mother informed me that cousin M____ has run off with Jeb. H. and that she was already with a child. But I can't, why? Why? Yes, the ship's doctor told me that it would take a miracle for me to conceive and deliver a live and healthy child. Yet, I have a dream that it does come true and James is happy and I too am happy.

Feb. 5, 1898

The snow is coming down and we needed more coal and James said that he had only two dollars left. He gave me one and I bought a small sack of coal.

Feb. 10, 1898

Our Sunday School took up a collection for James and it was over 15 dollars. My friend Annie McPhee must have passed the word around about James' needs. Philippians 4:19 *"My God will supply all your needs."* I do believe that! Most of the people who come to our classes are workers at the factories and with all the children they have even fifty cents is hard for them to part with.

March 30, 1898

I went to the city and saw all the pretty flowering shrubs. They are still digging for a tunnel for the cars to run from some place to another place. I told Dear James, NO I did not want to ride underground. I think it would make me sick like I was coming over in that ship and certainly scared. I again went to the library where they have magazines and books to read. So many you do not know where to start. I enjoyed the library but not the streets with horses and autos racing at break-neck speeds. Joe Puffer from Harrington, Maine and Edgar Jones are both helping James with our growing Sunday School as they learn more about Jesus.

March 31, 1898

A birthday – I am nearly finished with the second blue diary. One more year to go – I'll be 26 then. I sometimes wonder why I keep writing. I do find that I go back over my words and remember those good times that James and I have had. Well excluding that trip over the ocean it has been rather peaceful. We are a good pair, we think alike and when I am able to, I help him with all of my strength and mind. I thank God for James every day.

April 3, 1898

I have been sick in bed for nearly two weeks. James has done all the cooking and tending me. What a husband! My dear, dear James. The new Pastor came to visit with me. The house was a mess but I was very glad to have the Rev. George L. Collyer visit me. He is the right man to visit a sick and a somewhat discouraged woman. He listened to my story and was most sympathetic.

May 14, 1898

We all had a picnic in the park. James invited a lot of his fellow students. Hazen Baird from Amherst N.S., Fred Griffith from N.S., Gordon Ross from Greenhill, and Edgar Jones, Newfoundland, were the ones who thought up the idea. The senior class consisting of Frank Osgood, Don Piper, Will Patten and Fred Palladino came at James' invite. They all will do great things for the Lord. After we ate, Fred P. led us in some very good singing. Soon some of the strollers in the park came and started singing with us. At the end James gave a little sermon to the crowd. They applauded him. My husband is a very good speaker.

June 24, 1898

Classes are over and James will spend more time here in Hyde Park with the hope of increasing our numbers and also do more tailoring so that we will not be near begging every day for our food and shelter. Not that I have starved but we were cold this past winter for lack of coal. I will work every moment that my sickness allows for I am determined that more souls will be won in Hyde Park.

Letters from home. Mother did not ask her usual question, but sent a great deal of news about friends and relatives.

Aug. 1, 1898

The numbers of our Methodist Epworth League class and our Sunday School have grown and we have worked with the sole purpose to win more souls. We have and Praise GOD.

Sept. 3, 1898

James has gone back to classes to start the next term at the University. I am feeling much better now. And our Epworth League people are looking to me to lead them in a class. We will have two classes. Rev. George is a very good leader and we find him a friend.

Dec. 25, 1898

I have been too sick to enter my thoughts. James has been doing most of the housework. Today is my best for some time. I did go to church this week.

Jan. 2, 1899

We are near the 20th Century

James bought the newspaper again today. At the drug store all the men were in a tizzy. Some fool of a Senator was proposing that all the Union veterans even those who had skipped out of the service be given pension. Some of the veterans said that foolish Senator might even put in a bill to pension all of those poor southern men who had sent them to Andersonville. Andersonville was a prison that most blue Union soldiers never survived. This whole thing was in the newspaper. I could hardly belive what I read.

Jan. 7, 1899

The newspaper was full of those ridiculous predictions. I will list a few – 1. Automobiles will be cheaper than horses. 2. Liquefied air will keep food from spoilage. 3. You may soon be able to turn on cold or hot air in your house like hot and cold water. 4. Farmers will apply electric currents to the ground to speed up growth for plants. 5. Wireless telephone and telegraph will soon span the earth. 6. Instead of cavalry by horses, man will drive a huge mechanical fort at high speeds across open spaces in battle.

Feb. 10. 1899

Our money is nearly all gone and we need coal and food. Yet somehow we will make it through this cold weather and surely some of our friends will see our need. *"God will supply all our needs."* Philippians – Yes! Someone will see our need and God will touch them to help us. Thanks be to God.

Feb. 15, 1899

Rev. George Collyer came by with a most welcome gift of money. Coal and food that we needed during this snowstorm. The storm lasted two days here in Hyde Park – it has snowed without letting up. James measured it and said it was close to sixteen inches. Now that was a major storm.

Feb. 20, 1899

We had a caller from our Sunday School. He said they had met after church and all had added a half dollar to a collection for us. They knew we needed coal and we did. My dear friend Annie McPhee must have spread the word of our plight. Thanks be to them and to God. We are blessed with understanding friends.

Feb. 23, 1899

James has asked the local D.S. how he might contact one of the D.S. in the East Maine Conference. James has made up his mind to seek a regular appointment. He is

33

happy with the learning but not with my freezing and going without proper food.

March 2, 1899

James got a letter from a Rev. Jones from Maine. He is interested in having James take a church in Maine. His advice was for James to send him a history of his work in God's vineyard. And stay at the school until a church was found for him.

March 12, 1899

No work since Christmas at the tailor shop. Our purse is drained. James had saved while we were in Amherst but the cost to live in the U.S. is much too high. James is somewhat discouraged and has said that it might be a good idea to accept a call to some established church. We will pray about that.

March 24, 1899

The public library has been completed here in Hyde Park. It is a very impressive building. I have gone a few times to borrow a book. I got one of Mark Twain's as every one at the church is taken with it. Yes, it did have a message. He is saying God made us all equal in His sight.

March 31, 1899

Last entry – Another birthday – I looked for a new diary but they were too costly or not the right color. I want blue just like the first one.

Diary

~Bessie~

1899 – 1904

April 10, 1899

James came home with the blue diary and he said, "Don't ask what it cost." This is going to be my first entry. What changes since I first made my first entry in my first diary.

What a lovely spring day. When I am sick I think of days like this and I feel better. God made them all but I am very glad to have warm sunshine and flowers to see. They make my soul sing and I do. I'll go find Annie McPhee and we can have a duet for the neighborhood children.

April 15, 1899

The Rev. E.G. Jones wrote that the Bishop will soon send James a letter accepting him into the East Maine Conference and that a church will be found for James to Pastor.

April 20, 1899

I was glad to get a lot of news from mother. Father and the boys are doing fine. Courtney has another son called Vaughn. Rupert is a handful mother says. But she is glad to help take care of him when the new one came.

The ice is out early this year so they can plant their garden soon.

April 30, 1899

We just got the Bishop's letter and James has an appointment in Cushing. I asked, "Where is *that*?" James had asked to go into the field partly because we need a source of money to live. The congregation here at Hyde Park gave us a small sum most every week, but sometimes it would pay for food and none left to buy the coal when winter came. James went down to the Boston Library and discovered where Cushing was in the state of Maine.

James got quite a lot of work at the tailor shop because of Easter. *"For those who seek – will find"* and

James kept on stopping at Mr. Routley's shop until work was available. Thank God for all things.

May 2, 1899

The Dean, Marcus Buell, at the School of Theology asked James to come by and see him. So he went yesterday and the Dean had been looking at his file and when James came in the Dean said the President wanted them to come to his office. After they had sat down the Dean said, "So you were born in England in the town of New-castle-on Tyne?" James said "yes" and the Dean said, "Did you know that Anna Howard Shaw was also born there in 1847?" James said, "Yes, I know about the lady who graduated from the school several years back. We all heard and talked about her."

Then President William Warren said, "I have wondered if anyone at our school was aware of the magnitude of Anna Shaw's work. I am glad some has seeped down to the students of today." James did tell them that some of the professors and especially Dr. George Morris, had pointed out that women could and did graduate from the school to go on and become quite well-known. Then the President said, "Mr. Gray, Anna Shaw graduated with a degree and she was poor, poorer than Job's turkey. Why are you not staying the course?" James told him about my sickness and that he loved me too much to stay and have me eat crackers and water for another year or two. Then the Dean said, "Anna would have considered herself lucky to have crackers and water." I think I got this as James told it.

I wish I was as robust as my dear mother who could do the housework and help dear father in his business for hours at a time.

(Just a note of historical interest by author – the church records for the First Methodist Episcopal Church in Hyde Park can be found in six volumes 1906-1956 at Boston University Library. Last updated on March 5, 1997)

May 10, 1899

The Methodist class and the Sunday School took a special offering for us Sunday. It will be enough to buy the fare to Cushing and have five dollars and 23 cents left over. We will sell everything that we can't carry. It will be better to buy those things in Cushing. We did not have much when we came here and we leave with somewhat less. I will miss these ladies who have children by the dozens whereas I am barren. Mother wrote me a long letter about all the doings in Port Elgin. I will write her as soon as I arrive in Cushing. No, I think I'll do it on the train. I hope we have enough food in the kitchen to feed us on our way north.

May 11, 1899

The Methodist organization in Maine told James they will be sending us to an independent church in Maine. It has always had a Methodist pastor. I pray that they will welcome us to their community.

May 13, 1899

We look like the young immigrants that come to Boston carrying all their belongings. I carry his and my clothes in the coat that I had mended in Amherst. My dear James has our sleeping things rolled with his few books inside and his Sunday good shoes hanging around his neck by their laces.

I was glad that it was not raining and the walk from the local train to the North Station for our train was not too far. I had some food in my pockets and so did James.

May 14, 1899

We slept a bit last night as the train hooted and tooted and stopped at many villages and towns. We have a little food left for this morning's breakfast. We got off the train at Thomaston, Maine. And after making inquiries found the Rev. A.F. Wenchenback – the local Methodist minister

with whom we spent that night. He phoned the Brothers
in Cushing to inform them of our arrival.

May 14, 1899

Mr. A.S. Fales driving a decrepit freight wagon whose
wheels looked like they might just be ready to fall off,
came to the parsonage for us. Then we were driven over a
muddy-rutty and spine-jolting road until we came into
Cushing. I smelled the salt air and was hit with a wave of
home sickness. I know that James likes that smell and it
is not crowded with people here. It is a very small village.
WE ARE AT CUSHING.

A small white house near the church has been rented
for us. It will do. It has two rooms down and two up and
a small basement. Mrs. Brasher and Mrs. Harthorn had
filled the pantry with food. A bed with blankets, a few
chairs, dishes to cook and eat from. There was wood, part
of our pay, to burn and water to pump so we will be ready
for the Sunday service. Yes – what nice people!!!

May 20, 1899

We are finally settled after our much too long weary
train ride from Hyde Park. We bought more bedding and a
few dishes today. The parishioners had stocked the
kitchen with food and one old feather bed. I will wash the
tick and put in more feathers as soon as I find out where
the store is. A four-room home is very nice. It is all we
need to serve the Lord Jesus. This is a very small church.
About thirty people came the first Sunday to look us over.
I am sure the District Superintendent told them that
James is an Englishman and that I am a Canadian.

May 21, 1899

I joined the WCTU. I have seen enough of the evils of
liquor – Seamen drunk in Port Elgin.

May 23, 1899

James got paid today. This is going to happen every week. We are receiving $400 per year. That is not as large a sum as my father made in just a few weeks, but we are in a different type of work. We are in God's work. But it does feel good to know that now we can have wood to heat the house and food on the table every day. Albion Morse brings us wood from his boat yard. It is nice and dry. For when we were in Boston there were times when we had to choose one or the other. The fish is very good – just like home. I am feeling very good and well for this being by the sea is good for the body and soul.

June 10, 1899

James had his first funeral here at Cushing. D.B. Conant's granddaughter Julie Lowry had a baby at about six month pregnancy and the girl baby was born dead. I was called on to comfort her. I did and am glad even though for the next few weeks my nightly dreams carried me back to my loss. I cried out loud and had to hold James in my arms to comfort me. That sorrow and my bleeding started again. So now I must wash sheets every day.

July 4, 1899

I had sent a letter to Annie McPhee – I got her letter today. It was full of news. Uncle Gray had another fire at his mill. Mr. Frank McNuttly was killed in a train crash outside of Boston. I had met his wife the few times she came to class.

I have been given an old copy of the Sunday Globe. The United States is still at war even though they signed a peace treaty with Spain a year ago. In the Philippines, America lost five hundred men in just one battle. Pray to God that peacekeepers will soon solve the war in that far place. Parades here in Cushing. We had Mr. and Mrs. Wotton for Saturday's evening meal. He builds ships with his partner Jefferson.

August 2, 1899

Some of the young ladies and I went picking rapsberries today, and it was a lot of fun to be with them. They said we all should go pick blueberries later. We had the other clergy over for the evening meal. William Morse, the Baptist, is round and jolly. He and his wife Nat are very good at singing. Alex McGrover came as he fills in for the Advents. He is the town clerk. He is rather fun as a storyteller like the ones told in Port Elgin.

August 10, 1899

The schoolhouse needed repairs and James asked the Sunday School men and women to give the place some loving care. We had a picnic lunch and it was such a fine day the schoolhouse looks as good as new now. Jameson and Wotton furnished the material out of their well-stocked hardware store.

Sept. 10, 1899

We have had blueberries on our pancakes for several days and I made pies and jelly. If we are not careful we will each weigh two hundred pounds. A constant source of money and free blueberries are to be blamed. The barn has been finished so the members can have their horses protected from the winter weather. That was James' first request from the congregation. Without a barn only those quite near the church would come as soon as it got winter. We needed a place for James' driving horse. I think I will have a few hens in the barn. Fresh eggs are very good. Mother had a pig but I'll pass on that but a duck or two would be just fine.

Sept. 14, 1899

We had a blue clay pot given to us last Sunday after church. A potter, Mr. Barker Brook, said to me, "Now Bessie Dear, if you're living in Maine, you'll be baking beans on Saturday, and I make the best bean pot in this

here state, why to make one a heirloom I've put on the
letters G R A Y on both sides of this nice bean pot." I
thanked him very firmly.

The next thing was a Mr. Gould from Friendship sent
me a ten pound bag of his baking beans. Just a sample he
said in a note. In the bag I found a newspaper that had a
big write-up about a large -- no, he said it was the world's
largest -- paper mill. It was in Millinocket and again the
Americans always have the biggest and first on most any
subject.

Oct. 25, 1899

We went to a house blessing for the new home that
Captain J.A. Simmons built. Most of the community was
there. It followed that the Martin Browns at the Cove
would have us bless their house even though it was a
year old.

Nov. 30, 1899

We had a great church supper at the home of Mr. Fred
McClellan in his new home. He had taken the old one
apart and used the material and more to build him a
spacious and beautiful home. Each wife brought her best
dish, we had roast pork, roast beef, roast chicken and
some roasted lamb. Fish of many kinds. Lobster all red
and ready to dip in butter. Vegetables – beets, turnips,
carrots, potatoes, canned tomatoes, fiddleheads and
canned wild mushrooms. Yes, and there was a big bowl of
hazelnuts which are so very tasty. The cake and breads
were from chocolate to molasses cookies. The tables were
groaning. Nearly sixty people in all were very happy and
filled with good humor for we all sang afterwards for
nearly a half hour. A real thanksgiving meal and James
and I both gave short testimonials. While I was helping
clean up afterwards, and the men caught up on the latest
news, I let it out that the rented house was overrun with
mice.

Dec. 2, 1899

Sunday school has grown. We have 13 in the teenage class that I teach. Some of them ride their own ponies or horses to the church. I am planning to have a Christmas play and these young girls and boys will do it. It will bring their parents to church and James will make a visit later. I finally got the hang of it – baking beans in a pot. It is not the way we did at home. Now I use lots of good molasses and strips of salt pork and let them take their time.

Dec. 15, 1899

We have a gift, a rather young kitten in need of a home. It has very unusual coloring, striped red and white, like a peppermint candy cane. James said right out, "Candy" and that became its name. So we have a boarder and I hope it pays the fare by driving out those pesky mice.

As Christmas nears I'll miss my Hyde Park friends, especially Annie McPhee and her family. I am going to send a long newsy letter to them and ask them to pass it around to our many friends there. I hope they read it to all our friends.

Dec. 30, 1899

It was a lovely play and the girls did a very good job. I kept telling them to speak up like you do to your brothers so you can be heard. They did and even with a baby fussing in the back row in the church the people understood them. I thank my God for such a willing bunch of young girls. And I have almost stopped bleeding. Maybe, just maybe, I will get with child. It breaks my heart sometimes when I hold other people's babies.

Jan. 1, 1900

A new century. And many new things are coming, they say in the Boston newspaper. Some professor from Chicago was proclaiming that even if most of the newspapers have us entering the twentieth century, he says it is not true. This Professor says that when it was January 1 in year 0, we had not yet entered the second century from the birth of Christ. Well man's time and God's are not the same. Man marks time so he can keep the records accurate.

The newspaper had a long story about Japan and the great barging that had been made by some ambassador sent to make trading easier. Well they do have some nice things, but I'll never have the money to buy them. Annie wrote saying that the church was going to have a new pastor, The Rev. George L. Collyer.

Jan. 2, 1900

We had all the leaders of the church for a meal on Jan. 1. The house was a little crowded but a good time was enjoyed by all. Those scientists say that in the next hundred years Americans will be two inches taller. Now that is a strange thought – every 100 years Americans will grow two inches taller. They will soon have to rebuild all the houses and churches.

Jan. 5, 1900

A.S. Fales gave me his Boston Globe paper after he had read it. It had some old news about the professor in Chicago about when the twentieth century started. Time – God keeps time and mortals try. Now there was a story about the American navy in a far-off place called Japan. I just read a part of it. Then an article about Scott Joplin and his rag music, they told about his Maple Leaf Rag – I would rather listen and sing John and Charles Wesley's music. Another article that took my notice was some congressman said that all Union deserters should have a pension for some of them had fought battles before they took leave of the army. Then some wag answered that by asking if the good-hearted congressman wanted to give all Johnny rebels a pension from Washington. They are saying that man will fly not just in hot air balloons, but in heavier than air machines. Just like birds. And someone wrote that ships would cross the ocean in a few days driven by steam. I'll not take one even if it could cross in a day. Oh yes, soon no more horse cars in Boston – they will all run on electric power. I thank God I live in a little Maine town. I like horsepower.

Jan. 6, 1900

That newspaper had a report saying fewer people are coming down sick with Typhoid fever. For that I am glad but not for the many souls that went to get rich from California gold. Many lost their lives in that mad scramble.

Jan. 10, 1900

When it snows in Maine you think it will never stop. Well at least that is my thought on the last storm. It stormed for three days and the snow piled up and up by the back door in a three-foot drift. Candy has most of the mice under control. Only rarely do I find their droppings on my cupboard shelves. The newspaper reports we are on the gold standard. I wonder what that means. It also said they were sending messages through the air from one place to another without the wire that we have for the telephone. I cannot really think there are over 8,000 automobiles here in the United States. Why would you buy one of those machines? They seemingly are broken down by the road whenever we go to Thomaston for some of the things we cannot buy here. James has done some tailoring for a shop in Thomaston for a little extra...I think I hear James – he is back from Thomaston and the wagon wheels need grease. They are announcing his arrival – for they are squealing. He is very late for supper and I have spent too much time writing in my diary.

March 2, 1900

We now have a Sunday School and nearly every Sunday some thirty or more people in the congregation. I play the pump organ and some of them have pretty good singing ability. I am glad to do God's work in this rather backward area. It seems that almost half of the people cannot read very well. Yet they can all do their numbers because as one can see they are all prosperous. I am afraid we are going to have another family soon. Candy is heavy with kits. I wish I was. We have tried.

March 12, 1900

Rev. Jones, the District Superintendent sent a letter to James telling us of the conference meeting to be held in Clinton, Maine. We are both to go. Charles Smith wrote that he will see us there. Another train ride. It will be from April 24-29. We will get to meet all the Methodist ministers and their leaders. It will be our first and I hope that there will be many more.

March 30, 1900

About six inches of snow fell last night. James had to shovel most of the morning at the church and here. But when the sun does shine my husband will visit all the people of this area. If they are Baptist he pays a small quick visit but there are many without any church connection and James will try hard to win them for Jesus.

April 15, 1900

We have bought the tickets and have made arrangement with some Methodists to stay in their home in Clinton. The good Methodists of Cushing took up a special collection so we would not be without funds for the trip. Candy has three kits and they are cute but none have her markings. The District Superintendent sent a letter last week and told us the Bishop is going to send us to Rockport. It will be a bigger church and James found out that the parsonage has a nice barn so he plans on buying a new driving horse. Now he walks to do his visiting for the old horse is sick.

April 28, 1900

We left early in the morning for Clinton for the annual conference. We bought some food at the store to help out the good people that put us up in their home. They knew James at BU. They were very good hosts.

Bishop Isaac Joyce was a great leader and he preached a sermon that everyone will remember for a long time. I loved the singing. We sang old and new songs so everyone was happy. John Pinkerton and Charles Smith – James' BU friends – came to our place after dinner one night so we got better acquainted with them. Fred Palladino is going to Damariscotta Mills, Charles Morse to Columbia and Frank Osgood is going to Fort Fairfield. Charlie Jones to Easton. They sat with us at times. We enjoy these good Christian friends. I must write Annie.

April 29, 1900

Now we are home and must get ready to move. I enjoyed the singing and the preaching in Clinton. It would convert the devil. It was just glorious.

May 1, 1900

We have told the congregation that we will be leaving them. I did not have much chance to get to know them but I hope that God's seeds and our work will take firm root and grow. I have found homes for Candy's offspring. The mice have mostly moved out and so we will keep Candy, our boarder, when we move to Rockport. I sent Annie our new address with a small note.

May 2, 1900

James has bought a sturdy wagon and swapped his old horse for a small younger trotting horse. A pretty one – sorrel coloring. She is about six years old. She does not seem afraid of trains or the rare automobile that we meet. We will drive to Rockport and send what little furniture we have by Fales wagon. James has called the mare Maud. I like to ride beind her. She knows how to trot gracefully.

We have shipped the bed and dishes and now with some food we will go to Rockport in the morning.

May 3, 1900

We have eaten the oatmeal and are ready for **Today** is moving day. It will not be the last one. First to Amherst, N.S. then to Hyde Park, to Cushing, Maine, and now Rockport, Maine. James has all the furniture on the freight wagon. And with Candy, food and a change of clothes as needed, we are on our way. The roads may be dusty or rutted, but not muddy for it has not rained for a week. As we climbed up to the wagon seat I reminded James of that move out of Hyde Park when we sure looked like immigrants. Today we can pass as the Rev. James Gray and wife Bessie Gray. Praise God!

May 5, 1900

ROCKPORT

It rained on the way and the road is very rutted but our new horse, Maud, did an excellent job pulling us to Thomaston. We spent the night with the Winchenback family. James had met him at the conference and Mr. Winchenback had asked us to stop at their home for that night. In just one year their boy and girls have sprouted. On the way James stopped and pulled two automobiles out of the ditches. That is why I think they are an unneeded item...

It started raining as soon as we left Thomaston. But with our bonnet up we were mostly dry when we got to

Rockport. The locals knew where the parsonage was and so after we had stopped at a store to buy a few items of food, we drove to the Methodist parsonage. We found the parsonage is a larger home with a nice kitchen and a big new stove, and there are three rooms down and three up. It will look bare until we can buy more furniture.

Ralph Spear met us at the parsonage. I think he had hired someone to keep an eye out for us. He had a fire going in the kitchen and a teakettle on. James put Maud in her stall and we all had tea and some food from the basket I had packed.

May 6, 1900

Yes – the Bishop said we should have been here earlier but we had to do some things first...a better horse and wagon – yes – so we could bring our worldly things to Rockport to their nice parsonage. We now have a big cellar, a kitchen, pantry, dining room, living room and three bedrooms upstairs. Our furniture is lost in such a big house. And the barn, lots of room for those that come from the outlying farms and plenty of room for my hens. I will add a turkey and a few ducks.

July 3, 1900

I have heard the sound of cannons being fired now for several days. I thought the Americans were getting in practice for the 4th of July. When I went to buy some iron pills the doctor had ordered I asked the druggist, Mr. Champney, what all the celebration was about. He laughed and said, "Mrs. Gray, that boom you hear is no celebration but the sound of dynamite at the lime pit. Now if you go over to Rockland you will see a big, a very big, hole in the ground and that is where the farmers get their lime." So it was not practice session for the 4th of July. Candy has caught lots of pesky mice hunting in the house and out in the barn. She puts some by the door most every day.

July 4, 1900

These Americans surely celebrate the time they started their struggle to be free of Great Britain. A parade and bands from several communities came and marched down our streets. The bandstand had bunting and the audience sang along with the music sometimes. I would like to, but won't tell some of these cocky Americans that in Canada the women vote and in America they don't. That would never do, so I'll celebrate with them. Now we are here it is best not to flout my Canadianism.

James is finding that this town has a lot of backsliders and he says he will soon have many of them on their knees at the rail repenting. My flow of blood is rather small but some every day. If it stops maybe I'll get with child and then when I help at the church by holding a crying baby I'll not choke up in my heart.

August 5, 1900

Fresh fish and the money to buy. James is receiving $600 a year now. We are making a lot of new friends here in Rockport. The sea breeze makes this a good place to live if we only had a child we would be the happiest couple in America. Yet God has his purposes and it seems that mine from the beginning has been to be James' helper. Helper in winning souls for Christ. That we are doing, praise God!

August 12, 1900

I got tangled up in some bushes going after mushrooms and I could not seem to get my self upright. So I just sat down and waited for help. Well you never know who or when. But after quite some time a man came within my view and I yelled really loud and he heard me. Well, am I glad for Mr. Joe Abbott, our grocer, he came over and with his help I got up and was able to stand. He had come to gather mushrooms for his table. I thanked him and THANKED him. James would have had

to look – where – he would not have known. I might
have spent the night in that cow pasture. Thanks to Mr.
Abbott and my prayers, I did not sleep under the stars.

August 20, 1900

More kittens and they are cute but we will need to
find homes for them. I have visited a woman doctor –
Mrs. Weideman – she gave me some pills and said HOPE
for the Best. I am. The church is full nearly every Sunday
and we are happy in God's work. My hens are laying
more eggs than we can eat so I have started selling a few
each week.

Sept. 1, 1900

We had several local people, the Universalist minister,
Mr. and Mrs. Will Stow, Mr. and Mrs. Burpee, he owns
the casket store and does help in the funerals, Mr. and
Mrs. Bidwell, who works at the granite works. The eight
of us had a good time playing whist and singing songs
both the new ones and old ones.

Sept. 12, 1900

The high school principal and his wife came and had
supper with us. He and James came up with a plan to
bring more of his young students to our church. He is a
strong Methodist and wants the church to grow.

Sept. 20, 1900

With Ralph Spear teaching the young gentlemen
students and I the girls we have nearly sixty people
coming to the Rockport Methodist Episcopal Church.
Praise God.

Sept. 30, 1900

Frank Ingraham, the lawyer, has made James proud for
he was never in this church until James visited with him

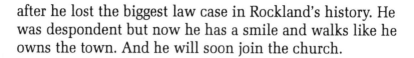

after he lost the biggest law case in Rockland's history. He was despondent but now he has a smile and walks like he owns the town. And he will soon join the church.

Dec. 1, 1900

Plans are underway for a visit by my sister, Reta, she is 19 now and not married. Ernest is 23 and has a family and is working with Courtney. Mother said that Courtney is acting like he was a millionaire. Maybe he is. Wrote a long letter to Annie.

Jan. 2, 1901

Well – I have read the newspaper and so many new things are happening – it makes my head spin. I have been well now for the whole month and it was so nice to have Reta here. Reta filled me in on the Jacob and Mira Dobson family and Calvin and Elizabeth Raworths.

I knew that Courtney had married Eldora Murray but we went over the children. Mother got it wrong sometimes. Rupert b. 1897, Vaughn b. 1899. We had several of the younger Christian boys and girls here for parties twice while Reta was with us. I thought she took a fancy to young Billy Hyde. They would have been an attractive pair, but Reta left for Port Elgin on the 30th of Dec.

March 31, 1901

We did the town up right good because my DEAR James, and he is a dear, took me out to dinner for my birthday at the best place in Rockport, the Hotel run by Mr. Lynde. We had a four-course meal, soup to nuts is what they say. Yes – and we did not go home right away for they had some musicians that played some waltz tunes that we both found very acceptable. A short note from Annie, a new minister at First Methodist, another George, this one the Rev. George F. Durgin. Boston has a Durgin Park. I wonder if that man is part of the family which the park was named after?

April 12, 1901

The newspaper says "Disaster" in bold headlines. We have had so much rain the last few days that the Penobscot River flooded and most of the bridges have been damaged. Trains have been stopped and the roads are awash with mud and water mixed with uprooted trees.

April 19. 1901

I got a letter from my dear friend in Hyde Park. The Methodist Church has more people joining. Most all the women in our part of Hyde Park have new babies. Annie named them all. I wish I could be there when they are baptized – and have one of James and mine be baptized.

April 21, 1901

I got a short letter from mother. Courtney has another boy named Roy. Tammy Copp, my schoolmate, died from Typhoid. Tammy was married and had five children. Mother complained about the heavy rains that knocked down trees and washed out roads. Mother does not usually say much about the weather. It must have been bad like we had here.

April 27, 1901

We took the train from Thomaston to Yarmouth for the East Maine Conference. The Bishop was so Irish in his speech that most of the Methodists probably did not fully know what he said. It was good to meet up with old friends Fred Palladino, Charlie Morse, Frank Osgood and dear Charles Smith. We had already been told that we would be serving in Rockport another year.

May 3, 1901

We were told at the conference to plan on staying in Rockport. We like it and I think most of the congregation is happy with us. Their numbers are growing. Charlie

Morse is going to serve in Columbia. Not too many other changes this year. Got a long letter from Mother. Reta is home and is being chased by an Oulton boy. Cora Silliker has moved to P.E.I., William Allen married Eva Robinson, John Dolye and Ernest Plummer have taken off to the western provinces.

June 3, 1901

Two members of our church, Mr. Palmer and Mr. Mather returned from a fishing trip and came by the parsonage and gave me twenty nice fat trout. I'll cook two for our supper and ice the rest until I can buy a few canning jars. I have done that when members gave us large cuts of good venison. James eats most everything but he is not so fond of some of the freshwater fish. These trout look very appealing.

June 4, 1901

The trout were very tasty and I have found the right size canning jars. School is out and I am going to organize some of my Sunday school girls into foraging for berries and other wild food. I will have a class telling them which mushrooms are safe to eat.

June 10, 1901

I have ten girls – teenagers – coming to the parsonage twice a week. We are having a botany course and will soon start eating fiddleheads and dandelions. We also have devotions before every field trip.

July 4, 1901

These Americans celebrate with another parade. I went as my girls are in the celebration.

July 11, 1901

James took me for a ride in the buggy. We tour the area and visit the Samoset Hotel. It is certainly a grand one and must be very expensive. We will not be partaking.

July 14, 1901

We are still having class for the girls. I suggested the same for the boys but soon discovered that they are helping in their family or have jobs. I really do love my young girls. Any one of them would be a daughter to be very proud of.

July 20, 1901

We were invited to the Mitchells, he is the Adventist minister. The Walkers came, he is the Episcopal minister. The Mitchells have two young girls 14 and 16 that acted as our waiters. We all applauded them for doing a good job. They are Sue and Mary and both asked me as we were leaving if they could come and join my Methodist girls – I said, "If your father approves I would be pleased to have you."

Aug. 28, 1901

What a storm last night. It blew many shingles off roofs all over town. The lightning was most severe. A barn out toward the corner of Spear Road and Hovey was struck and burnt. I saw the smoke! We did not lose any shingles but the church did. Some of the fishing boats were damaged. Many trees have been uprooted. Maud kicked a hole in the side of her stall, she must have been quite nervous about the crashing thunder and the wind blowing. James will need to buy some boards to fix the stall. It will be a few days before they have it all cleaned up.

Sept. 15, 1901

I bought some early rose potatoes yesterday. They were put in burlap sacks in Caribou by Cory Powers. I will write him that I liked them very much – so tasty. I read the headlines in the newspaper that said, "A new mechanical horse will soon be hauling the logs." It's called a Lombard and they said it will revolutionize the wood industry. This summer weather has the birds confused. They should be going but there are many geese that are still here on the ponds.

Nov. 10, 1901

A letter from mother and she says Reta has finally agreed to marry Avery Oulton of Baie Verte. He works for Courtney in the mill. Ernest now has a boy named Victor. Courtney lost a son, Roy, he had contracted smallpox and lived less than a few months. I sent a letter right off to my brother expressing our grief over his loss. I am always sick at heart on hearing of the loss of children. It tears at my fiber and I become sick.

Dec. 2, 1901

We have laid the plans to have a really fine Christmas pageant with my girls and Ralph Spears' boys. I was under the weather for over two weeks after hearing of Courtney's loss.

Dec. 15, 1901

We have rehearsed them and they are very good. I am going to invite the editor of the Rockland newspaper to come to our next rehearsal. I hope he will tell all his readers how very good this pageant is going to be. James says that we should plan on an afternoon performance and an evening one. The pageant is the story of "Oliver Twist" by Dickens.

Dec. 19. 1901

The Editor came and watched our rehearsal, Mr. Folger, and he was most generous with his praise.

Dec. 21, 1901

The Rockland paper had a very prominent article about my players. Mr. Folger was sent a thank you as soon as I had read it. This story puts the Methodists on the front page.

Dec. 27, 1901

We had a very large turn-out. The church was full for both performances. It was good to show and more people know about us Methodists now! I sent another note to the editor saying thanks again.

Dec. 31, 1901

When it snows here we measure it in feet. James spent all day shovelling it. My hens need culling. No point feeding those that don't lay, so we will have chicken soup. Oh! That reminds me of some of the first entries in my old blue diary. Before I married James. I'll have to find it and relive those days when I was full of plans and hope to serve the Lord Jesus in Africa. Oh! yes and to make soup for James. I'll have to tell him that story while he is spooning in my tasty hot chicken dumpling soup. Soup, yes, we had thin soup in Hyde Park, but not like this one we are making now. The McPhees' have a new boy, they call him Leo Jr.

Jan. 30, 1902

I have been sick for nearly a month with my bleeding. Poor dear James had to hire a woman to come take care of me and the housework. Mabelee Artwater lives with her sister here and had time to tend me. She has done this before and so she had a little knowledge of what to do. I am still not totally recovered. Now she comes twice a week to help me.

March 3, 1902

My health has returned and I am back doing God's work in the community. There are some children that need clothing and we ladies of the Methodist church collected a good lot for both boys and girls. The town will help people with food but not clothing to keep them warm. Mabelee comes by now quite often and we have tea and good fellowship.

April 28, 1902

We took a train and went north to Caribou for the annual conference of the East Maine Methodists. We spent one night in Bangor on the way. Stayed at the Bangor House.

It was the best hotel we have stayed in. The dining room was just marvelous and we ate some very good crab meat and slept in the best of beds. James and I both bought shoes – he one pair and I two pairs. Then for me a new blue gown that I just could not pass up. We left early in the morning but this train stopped at every small village. We got to Caribou very late at night. Took a cab to the hotel and quickly went to bed. We walked around this thriving town and found that they had many types of stores. I bought a hat at one of them located in the Arnold block.

Some of the many Methodists we met were the Polards, Little, Hale, Hight, Gray, Scott and Mrs. Stitham. Many more that I have forgotten. But I will remember Mr. Cory Powers and his nice wife. I told Cory how much I like his potatoes. They were very nice to me, gave me a bag of potatoes to bring home.

This town is surely going to grow and even though it is far from the sea I think we could be quite happy here. We did stop again on the way back from Caribou and spent a night in the Bangor House. It was worth the money even if we have to skimp a bit in Rockport I will just pick more wild fruits and other foods of the forest. I will go to the dock and buy my fish. I can clean them at home. Train travel is better than going by boat even if they sway and sometimes do little bumps between the click clicks.

The worst thing about riding the rails is the coal dust and black smoke that keeps you feeling grimy.

May 1, 1902

May day. This is the time we hung May baskets in Port Elgin. I hung one on the door of Royal Andersen when I was ten. He kissed me when he caught me. A child's kiss. I wonder what those old classmates are doing. Well some are married with lots of children, some have gone to western Canada to seek their fortune. Some have without a doubt come to the states as we have. And James' brother Sam, he never writes and James says where would he write to – general delivery but what town and country. Uncle Calvin Raworth, the one that married Elizabeth Allen, the redhead Allen, died. Mother sent me a short letter.

July 4, 1902

Mabelee and her sister Grace came over to have the noon meal with us. It being the fourth, they had seen the town's parade before they came. We got the whole of it, told first by Grace and then Mabelee. Just as good as standing and watching with your feet hurting. They were really quite enthused by all of it. I asked them if they had ever taken part in a 4th of July parade. Well they had several other parades to tell about.

August 1, 1902

I enjoyed the letter from Cushing, Mrs. Brasher wrote about the new pastor and how much she misses James' style of preaching. Well most people will find out, my James is one of the best preachers the Methodists have here in Maine.

August 12, 1902

My Sunday school girls and I have picked strawberries, and now we are going blueberrying. I have canned several quarts of both and James has eaten so many shortcakes that he will turn into a strawberry. But we both like that fruit.

August 25, 1902

Well the first time I have ever seen a black bear in the wild. I have seen them when their owner showed them off in some parade but in the wild is surely different. We – my girls and I came upon one in the blueberry field. It stood up and looked us over and we dropped our pails and raced from that field to the road. James said we did wrong, we should have made some noise and then walked away. Well the bear probably ate our picked berries. I will be back but to a different part of the field.

Sept. 12, 1902

School starts and I am going to find a really moving Christmas play for these girls of mine. I know they can do a very good job of projecting their voices. I heard them when we running away from that big tall ugly black bear in the blueberry field.

Nov. 2, 1902

The magazine that I borrowed from the library had an article about the settling of the Panama Canal. England handed over her part ownership, which was also to be a privilege for the Canadians, to the United States without any compensation. The Canadian Premier was quite put out with England. Then the British representative in the dispute concerning the boundary between Canada and the States sided with the Americans.

Nov. 30, 1902

My young girls are doing marvelously on the Christmas play. The boys need to raise their voices. I will talk to their leader. Candy has presented us with another batch of kittens. We will find them homes with some of our congregations. Mother wrote the news of Port Elgin. A day ago got a letter from Annie McPhee of Hyde Park, my dear friend has lost a son to the ravages of Scarlet Fever. I have written her.

Dec. 30. 1902

Christmas has come and gone and my girls really did a very commendable job presenting the play. The message was well received. This year has seen James do several funerals and I could not tell you how they affected me. So many young boys and girls died from something that they catch somehow, some from T.B., some pneumonia, many from smallpox and many others. I pray that this talk of a vaccine for these baby killers will come to pass. The Lord must be encouraging those research people to do this for all mankind. For this I will pray daily.

May 5, 1903

The trip was in a cold spell. The temp during the night was in the teens and in the day it was just above freezing.

We have arrived at Boothbay and my what a nice parsonage and stable. Candy was right at home very soon in both the house and barn. We will need to buy a few things. I hope dear James has a little extra money for me beyond the needs of food. James needs a new coat and two new shirts. The stores look inviting here.

May 27, 1903

We are making this our new home with new friends to make. Boothbay Harbor is a small village where some people fish and some make boats or ships. They harvest ice and some say it's the best money maker of all the endeavors. It reminds me of Port Elgin. But with some new things – a phone and electric lights. A small coal furnace down in the cellar which also heats our water. James has a small barn for his horse and we could keep a cow. I don't milk and James would not either. So we will buy our butter, cream and milk. A few hens for eggs. James' salary is very good – $850 dollars a year. When James told me that sum I asked him for a nice new hat to go with the blue dress I got in Bangor. He bought it for me.

June 3, 1903

I bought a dozen year-old layers from a farmer named Joe Skidgel. I have been making chicken soup from the older hens. I sure find this village interesting, quite a lot more stores and always a fresh sea breeze. Like HOME! I have not been sick for a week. Maybe this sea air will make me well. God willing.

We are stuck right out into the sea. The sea breeze has the smell of Port Elgin. We have a nice parsonage, four rooms down and two up. My hens have adjusted to the move and so has Candy, new mice to chase and catch. Maude has a small but comfortable barn. The hen house had to be cleaned and disinfected. It was lousy and that would make my hens poor layers. We have two doctors in our congregation – Dr. Blossom and Dr. Carter. Mr. Luce has the apothecary. Isaiah Lewis brought us wood for the kitchen and coal for the furnace.

June 12, 1903

James has laid plans with the leaders of the church to have a revival as soon as school is out.

My young ladies and Mr. Fisher's boys will act as ushers for the revival. Mr. Fisher has a dry goods store.

June 15, 1903

Ora Samuel Gray, James' brother fell out of the blue on us, and J.J. Jewett came and are staying with us for the next week. It is strange to have James' brother staying with us. They stayed up half the night talking and learning about each other's life and work. They are all excited about the many people that they will win in this town for Christ. The East Boothbay Methodists are going to help with this revival. They have no pastor at this time. The District Superintendent hopes to send someone soon.

June 17, 1903

I wish I had Mabelee here to help with the cooking and washing of clothes. Two extra is a strain on my constitution.

June 28, 1903

The revival services were very well attended and we will have several new Methodists at our church. James will take them into membership the first Sunday of the month.

July 21, 1903

James preached a morning sermon and I started the Sunday school with songs. I love to lead the children as I play the pipe organ. It is the best I have ever played.

(This organ is on the New England list of Historical pipe organs. Author's comment: "They played it for us on our visit. James and Bessie sang with this organ.")

I like it better than pump organs which were always out of tune. The evening service will be a time to give our testimonials. I will be telling of my love of Jesus and how much I like working in God's garden. The young Hodgdons are coming over this afternoon and I will invite them to stay for the evening meal. My new blue dress and a hat makes me look young and full of life and I feel that way right now. God has been good to me and my sickness

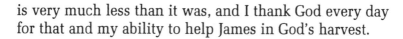
is very much less than it was, and I thank God every day for that and my ability to help James in God's harvest.

Aug. 30, 1903

The church was full Sunday and the evening service was also well attended. James is a very able and powerful preacher. He tells them of the pathway to blessedness and how Jesus will guide them through the perils of life. It is a rapture to my soul every time I hear him from the pulpit. The young Hodgdons came by last Saturday, Robert and Stella. They are telling us about the big fire of 1886 and how Fred Harris tried to get the people awake. He became hoarse for weeks after. The pumper was not able to do anything for quite awhile until finally someone came who knew how to run the thing. I'll tell more of that story after I digest it or find a printed account. Stern Robert and fiery Stella correct each other so many times that I'm going to seek an old newspaper for the truth about that fire.

Sept. 3, 1903

After reading about that old fire at the library I read the latest paper and found that the state had a forest fire which destroyed 268,000 acres of good woods. Once they start they are very hard to put out.

Sept. 10, 1903

THE WATER WORKS

My, those old newspapers, *Register* and its new name under new ownership, *Boothbay Register*, are very much for or against the water project. That fire got a lot of business people all concerned about the high insurance rate they would have to pay on their business. So they started out with the idea that a water supply was the answer. That caused the town people to be for it and the out-of-town people to be against it. So Boothbay, the old town, was split up. I discovered that cost was the problem and when it was all finished the cost was twice what they had planned on. Now I can see why some of the people that come to our church seem very unfriendly with some others. It goes back to that fire and then the fight over water to lower the insurance cost. But the water system for the town of Boothbay was slow in getting built. It was passed by the town meeting in Boothbay in March 5, 1894. The old hostilities are still very evident. James needs to preach about forgiveness.

Sept. 30, 1903

Now all the sons and daughters of Silliker and Millicent Raworth are married. Ernest, my baby brother, married Minnie Johnson Sept. 16, 1903 by the Rev. W.A. Thompson in the Raworth home. Mother said a large number of cousins came and some of the townspeople. I will write them a note soon.

Nov. 30, 1903

We decided to have a few of the good people of Boothbay Methodist Episcopal church at our table for Thanksgiving. So I invited Bob and Stella Hodgdon, Mr. and Mrs. Milton Rowe, the Kenneth Richards and Mr. and Mrs. Alonzo Nickerson.

I had hired a woman, Mrs. Lila Brown, to come and help prepare and serve the meal. We ate at about six in the evening so those who had to tend to business could come.

We had a very good time and I think that if we are here next year that I will invite some of those who were opposed to the water system. They will be mostly farmers or live out in the country from Boothbay Harbor.

Dec. 3, 1903

I have been mostly unable to help James for some time. I have put off doing my diary.

Dec. 10, 1903

A sad note from mother – Courtney's newest baby boy was stillborn early. A sad Christmas for them and I will be feeling their pain for my nightmares will surely return with this news.

Dec. 30, 1903

I am bleeding again and my nightmares are about that ship in the ocean that tosses me about and then they toss my newborn boy overboard into the frothing-raging-black sea. I wake up screaming and James has to hold me and comfort me. O Lord, I pray for deliverance from this nightmare.

Jan. 3, 1904

Lots of snow was shoved from around the church before James gave an inspiring sermon Sunday on the need to forget and forgive. He was aiming it at both sides of that water fight. I saw some old adversaries shaking hands as they left the church. Praise God! May they all become great forgetters and forgivers! I was only mildly sick this last week. I spent Thursday in bed with my sickness.

April 9, 1904

We took the train to Pittsfield for the conference. Bishop John Vincent was most forceful in his talks, and when he gave his sermon that Sunday morning why even the Lord would have been moved. He really did make the love of our Savior Jesus Christ feel so real that it touched your heart and made you jump with joy to be a Christian. We are home again and my cat Candy sure is glad. She had to live off mice for a few days and she really likes the table scraps best. Mostly she piles the mice up at the door to show us that she is worthy of her board and room. Our friends Charles Smith is at Sheepscot, while Fred P. is going to Caribou, Charles Jones to Easton. Hi Holt is going to Rockport.

May 24, 1904

We have been over to preach at the East Boothbay church most of this year. The District Superintendent said when the seminary in Bangor was out he would find a young student to fill that need.

June 3, 1904

The D.S. Rev. F.T. Jones sent a young student, Mr. James Swift. We had him over as soon as he came. He will need to find a boarding home in East Boothbay. We have him until that is accomplished. I did think he looked too young, too young to be a pastor. James was a man when he became a pastor.

June 30, 1904

We are going to have revival services. Mr. Swift and two others from the seminary are here to help James do it. I will be playing our great pipe organ for the revival.

July 4, 1904

We started the revival on this date. Our theme was "The Nation will accept Christ if you present Him."

July 12, 1904

The church was standing room only for the whole week of revival. Many joined the Methodist church – some East Booth or Boothbay. The three young men did such a good job. I am going to write the school and tell the headman what his great student did for Jesus Christ in Boothbay.

Sept. 4, 1904

We are planning to have a joint meeting with the leaders of the two churches. Mr. Swift goes back to school and James will have to do two services – one here and one there. We need to get the time right so our trusty mare Maud can cover the distance there in plenty of time. Word came from our DS about the tragic Typhoid epidemic in Bangor. They blame the water from the river for the problem.

Dec. 20, 1904

My usual letter from Hyde Park came today. I had written Annie my letter. She had lots of news about those good people of Hyde Park. A new minister at church – they like him and he has a wife and two boys.

Jan. 1, 1905

A new year and I will try to do more in my Diary. We did have snow for Christmas and James and I worked diligently for the good of the Methodist church in Boothbay. We had several groups over for an evening and some of the local pastors. But I was too busy to do my Diary.

Jan. 5, 1905

I bought James two new shirts out of my egg money for Christmas. Christmas was so rushed that my diary had very few entries. When there are no children to buy presents for our tree looks bare. So I bought him those shirts. Was he surprised and pleased.

A new year and – and the things that I have heard! Francis Greene, who is not noted for telling fibs, in confidence told James that Stella and Bob are having problems. He asked James to visit them. Bob moved in with his mother after his father died and left him the wholesale lobster business. Stella would not move into her mother-in-law's home. James is visiting both of them tomorrow.

Feb. 10, 1905

We got a letter telling us about the conference in April at Bangor. Found a store that had those good potatoes that Cory Powers raises. James is pleased with his Maud, she stays put when he visits people and never acts up when the train toots at a crossing.

Feb. 16, 1905

James has been praying with Bob and Stella over their problems. Stella says that one of the reasons she will not move in with old Mrs. Hodgdon is that she could not have marital relations with Bob because the old Mrs. Hodgdon was always spying on them when they were courting and she'd be doing the same if they moved into that old Hodgdon house. Bob had built them a very modern one before they were married. Bob says that he needs to be with his mother to help her in her infirmities. He is an only child.

Feb. 23, 1905

We have been told to plan on a move and James said that maybe it was time to take another charge. He hopes to get the Hodgdons back doing the right things.

March 10, 1905

Bob Hodgdon has told James he will get a divorce from Stella unless she comes to live with him. He says he is going to sell his house so Stella better make up her mind that she better move in with him and put up with his mother who will not live much longer anyway. James has pleaded with Stella to no avail.

March 18, 1905

Mother could have sent a telegram saying Father had passed away on March 2. She is too conservative to do that. I must take after her for I do not plan on riding in that automobile unless I am dead. Well mother said Father

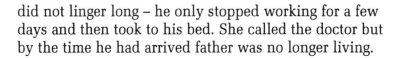

did not linger long – he only stopped working for a few days and then took to his bed. She called the doctor but by the time he had arrived father was no longer living.

April 15, 1905

The winter has gone and spring is showing its head. I am going to plant a small garden. Doctor Blossom said that some outdoor work will help my sickness. It sometimes becomes unbearable but I never complain to James. He has his own sickness that acts up much too often.

April 23, 1905

We have gone to the conference. It was in Bangor this year. The Bishop was Rev. Goodspell and he had a good spell over us. We met our fellow workers there, Charles Smith – who is going to Rockport. Fred P to Caribou again – Charlie Jones again to Easton. We did quite a lot of buying to refurbish our wardrobes. We ate at the Bangor House with Charles Smith and Charles Jones and Fred P. We have a pay raise!! James is going to be paid $900 a year. The Bishop said they had changed their minds about the move.

May 1, 1905

Trouble – Bob H. sold the house and Stella had to move and kind-hearted James asked her to come spend the summer here with us in the spare bedrom. I hope she can find a place to stay before fall comes. I would like to have my brother Ernest and his wife Minnie come and visit and we would need that spare bedroom. Ernest and Minnie Johnson got married on Sept. 16, 1903, mother wrote, and Courtney has a girl named after me, Bessie, born in 1905.

June 6, 1905

Our local politician was in town at the Post Office when James was getting our mail. He was expounding on the idea that all the big forest owners should build a tower in their forest on a high mountain so that small fires could be discovered and put out. It would save money for them he postulated. And he said up on Squaw Mt. the Shaw company had put one up to protect their trees.

July 4, 1905

The church is having a picnic. I did not go. I begged off as my sickness just overpowered me. James and Stella have left and I have a letter from my brother, Ernest. He is coming to the States to work in Boston. He said he would come early and visit us first. James is praying that he can get Bob and Stella back together. She told James that every time she sees Bob she wishes he would leave his mother and climb into her bed. She asked if James would invite him for an evening meal. And she confided in me that she was considering sneaking into Bob's bed some night after old Mrs. Hodgdon had retired.

Dec. 26, 1905

What a present we received. James had the funeral for old Mrs. Hodgdon the day before Christmas. Stella and Bob have made up. I found out then that Stella had visited Bob more than once while she stayed with us. James and I settled that marital lovemaking as soon as he was working in Amherst. Twice a week, Monday and Thursday, so it would not get in the way of the needs of the work. Stella confided that she would only be satisfied with once or twice each day!! But Bob was not up to that she had discovered. Well she has now moved into the old Hodgdon house. Bob will have to make some improvements I am sure and he will want to find some food to make him more virile. Our house seems empty now that Stella is gone, but I find that I enjoy being with James without company. I have written too much about Stella and Bob, but when someone moves into your home – WELL!

Brother Ernest did not come to America but took a short trip to Quebec City.

Dec. 30, 1905

The D.S. came today and slept in Stella's room. There I go. It's not Stella's, it's our spare bedroom. Visiting for our quarterly conference. I had the anti-water people for a harvest supper and made a lot of new friends. We invited all the local pastors to our house for a New Years time. I'll ask Stella to come help with the preparation and two of the teenage McFarlane girls, June and Jane, the twins, to help serve the meal. I'll serve roast beef and baked potatoes with lots of creamed carrots from the cellar. Stella can make a mince pie, the Stofords gave me the meat for it. We should have a few steamed clams with butter to start with. We are having six couples so I'll need a table from Stella, and a few chairs. The D.S. decided to stay for the party. Another plate and a chair.

Jan. 2, 1906

What a good time we had on New Years eve. We played a few games and then we sang many songs – some church ones and some that the Unitarian Minister, Mr. Frank Bell, said were new on Broadway. He has a great voice and led us most graciously. It was after midnight before they all left. Candy spent the evening in the clear and when I opened the door in the morning she had placed three large fat mice on the first step. Earning her keep!

Feb. 12, 1906

I have been in bed and out for two weeks now and I am going to Portland to see some special doctor that Dr. Blossom thinks can help me with these terrible pains I have.

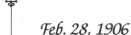
Feb. 28, 1906

The pills do make the pain bearable. I did not think I would have been gone so long from James but I had to wait for an opportunity to see the doctor for seven days. He had gone to Boston to attend a seminar on women's medical problems. Then we had a severe storm which delayed him. Then another storm hit Portland and I did not want to chance the train in such a storm – so I stayed put. I did not worry about dear James for my friend Stella said that she would tend to his needs. When I got back our house was all spiffed up – floors waxed and the furiture polished. Stella was here.

April 3, 1906

The district Super came to Boothbay and spent the night with us. The bishop has not told the District Superintendent his plans. That cat Candy has just presented us with another family. They are a lot of company, cute and playful but we will find homes for them. We must have Bob and Stella over for a visit.

April 30, 1906

We traveled by train, trolley and ferry to Vinalhaven for the conference. Bishop David Moore is not very good at preaching nor can he lead a song. Yet he has a very pleasant personality. He came to eat with us one evening after we had both given our testimonials at the love feast. He congratulated James and I on our testimonial. He then told us that he wanted us to stay one more year at Boothbay. We ate with the Charleses and Fred P. one night at the conference. It is great to greet old friends each year and hear about the souls they have saved. We have never missed an East Maine District Conference. James has been saying very forcefully that with railroads and automobiles becoming more available to everyone that we Methodists should be thinking of just one Maine Conference. He is not alone in this for it has been shown in other areas that it would save money in administrative costs. We are going to stay on at Boothbay one more year. We are both happy.

May 22, 1906

This country has become one of the leaders in the world. The canal and the Spanish war have made the States equal to the other leading nations. I hope it is for the good. I have not gotten interested in their politics as I still feel like a Canadian at heart. The church has grown under dear James and some of the water fight seems to have been forgotten or they don't show it as much as when we first came. I think I'll have both the "for water" and "against water" for a picnic on July 4. That's a big holiday in Boothbay. I'll get Stella to help me. Maybe Bob will furnish the lobster. Why, I think I'll ask him to boil them for us.

July 6, 1906

My, what a feed we had of lobsters. Twenty people (not all were Methodist – for I had asked the Bells) and forty lobsters. We had ice cream and strawberries for dessert. We did some singing before we ate and then we all joined in a full-blown choral concert. The weather was most cooperative. The crashing thunderstorm came smashing down on us just after the men had cleaned up from cooking the lobster and clams outside in the backyard.

July 10, 1906

James came home with the Portland paper and on the front page was a big warship, a battleship, the USS Georgia, being put into the river at Bath. The Americans are being militant. Who are they going to fight? They have already beaten Spain. Who else needs to be beaten in war?

Sept. 14, 1906

School is in and I have twenty young ladies in my Sunday School class. I can tell that this class will do something special for the Christmas celebration. Check 2nd Timothy 2:15.

Nov. 30, 1906

We had Bob and Stella for Thanksgiving and they brought their stereoscopic cards and viewer. They had bought a series that showed the Holy Land as it is now. James said if we ever came into a fortune that we would go to Palestine. Stella did the bread, cakes and pies and I am afraid we ate too much for our own good.

Dec. 10, 1906

The steamboats have stopped for the season. A lot of summer people come here by boat from Boston and New York.

I had sent a Christmas letter off last year to my dear Annie in Hyde Park. I was surprised when I got a letter with bad news. Annie had succumbed to pneumonia on July 1, 1905. Leo – just could not write that to me – so his sister came and read my letters and sent me this bad news. I sent Leo my sympathy.

April 24, 1907

We are in Hartland. We came on the S and M railroad and crossed the Sebasticook River. I was pleased with our trip to the Conference in Bar Harbor. We had good food and our stay at some friends of the Bishop was most delightful. What a large house. Ten rooms and two indoor bathrooms. I thanked Bishop Henry Warren and the Van Kiltons our gracious hosts. We visited with John Watson who is the pastor in Bar Harbor. Some of the assignments were Fred P. to Caribou, Charlie Jones to Linneus, and James to Hartland. I had to ask him where that was. James likes the barber Mr. Burton. We are going to bank at the Waterville Trust.

May 7, 1907

I had been surprised when we were told that we were going to leave Boothbay. I loved being able to breath salt air, but Hartland is far far from the sea. But the Bishop said that we were needed there. Now we packed a lot more things, for Boothbay has been good to us for which we are thankful.

May 10, 1907

How great to have Bob and Stella help us pack and now tomorrow we shall have to say goodbye to these good friends. God bless them. We have sold the wagon and horse. Dear James was quite attached to Maud, a dapple gray mare that knew her business. She could stand in the yard while James visited without getting restless. Maud came home many times when dear James had fallen asleep from too many long days.

May 12, 1907

We came to Hartland on the train. They are better than they were – a lot less smoke and cinders. We had the cat, Candy in a wicker basket and she remained very quiet and nice all the way. Mr. J.S. Norton met us with his very good-looking four seater wagon. It was polished and the matched pair of black Percherons were beautiful. They took us to a large house with six nice rooms, a cellar and an open attic.

May 13, 1907

This town has a large woolen mill like Port Elgin but it sits on a river, the Sebasticook. They keep reminding us that we are in Somerset county.

May 14, 1907

The Grace Linn, also called the Hartland church was named in honor of Mrs. Grace Linn. In 1871 the Methodist Society met at the Hartland Academy. It was the Linn and Buck families who pushed and worked so hard for a church building. The congregation named it after Mrs. Linn. I have been told the very first service in the Grace Linn church was the funeral for the dear lady. It is a handsome building.

May 15, 1907

We got settled in when our beds and bureau arrived yesterday. James has found a small wagon but he has not found the right horse yet. We have a small barn and could keep hens and a cow. I think I'll have the hens and buy the milk. Letter from mother finally caught up with us. Sister has a new baby boy, Avery Oulton Jr. and Ernest took time away from his work in Courtney's wood working to go visit the Ralph Murrays who have moved to Saint John to work for the newspaper.

May 20, 1907

We found out that J.S. Norton was the Superintendent of Schools and a rather new member of the Grace Linn Church. James has found a horse. It is not as nice looking as Maud, but James says she is well-trained. He calls her Dolly. I found the best fruit and meat market and it just happens that the owner, Fred Wyman, sings in the Grace Linn choir.

May 28, 1907

The Linn Woolen Mill makes shawls and cassimeres. "What," I asked James, "is that?" He said, "It is twill weave suiting fabric." Now I know. James is very busy and I have mostly got the house arranged the way I would like. Now I will plan on having the young people of the church come to the house for a party of singing and eating. We have a small musical instrument I can play. Courtney sent me a good check and said, "Buy what you like, sister." I have met the Baptist minister, Rev. H.L. Calkins, at the book and stationery store today. We passed pleasantries. I got a letter from Stella. She and husband are doing fine. He did remodel the old Hodgdon house.

July 5, 1907

We had a very impressive July fourth parade in town. The State guard and the Civil war veterans marched rather regally in the hot sun. Sunday school has a large number of children and adults. I think I will suggest that some class come to the parsonage for their meeting – the young teenagers that I'm teaching.

July 8, 1907

We need a few repairs to the front and back doors. Charles Lovejoy came and did a very excellent job. They look as good as new ones.

Aug. 2, 1907

I have discovered that they have a nice Library here. Miss Helen Linn is the Librarian. She told me she is the granddaughter of Grace Linn, the woman the Methodist church is named after. I asked her if she would come to supper Thursday and tell us about her grandmother. I took out a membership in the Library and took home some good reading. I may find solace in these books from that ache that my body has most of the time. James has a horse and wagon. An automobile is way too costly and who would dare drive on these roads. Every day some daring man tips his automobile over and has to be tended to by a doctor. We have two and they are busy – Dr. Baker and Dr. Moulton. I'll see Dr. Moulton if this pain does not cease.

Aug. 10, 1907

Dr. Moulton sent me to the druggist, Mr. Blanchard. Now I am feeling slightly less pain. The church is in a nice building and I think some of the people who come are just looking to see what Linn's wool has done for the town of Hartland. Miss Linn came again and she had a very interesting story about her family. I will think about it and add it to my diary soon.

Aug. 12, 1907

Mr. Webber and Mr. Miller, the town's select men, are proposing a speed limit in town of five miles per hour. They say many people are being injured by speeders.

Aug. 15, 1907

Archibald and Grace came to America in 1860 from Scotland. They brought with them machinery and workers to establish the Linn Woolen Mill. A devout Methodist, Mrs. Linn started immediately to organize a Methodist church. Soon she had a growing congregation meeting in her home. She then started raising money for a church building. Archibald was the first contributor. With some small help the Linn family finished the building in 1884. The first service in the church was Mrs. Grace Linn's funeral. The Church was dedicated in 1884 as **The Grace Linn Memorial Methodist Episcopal Church.**

Sept. 3, 1907

We have twenty young girls in my Sunday School class. They are 12 to 16 in age and they are all in school. The first meeting Jane Hill came but she has gone to Manchester to work in the cotton mills. Many girls have gone there to work. They write home and tell of their living under very strict rules. I asked Jane to write me.

Oct. 12, 1907

My hens are laying so many eggs that I will have to take some to the store for swapping. The Library is a great place to meet people that you never meet in church. Mrs. Brown, one of the Unitarians in town, is so nice. Her husband is the Postmaster. She is going to join our Book Club. We discuss the books we read.

Oct. 26, 1907

I am going to read Willa Cather's book "Wait till the Sun Shines Nellie." Mrs. Baker will read "The Chocolate Soldier," by Oscar Strauss. Mrs. Moulton will read Mark Twain's "A Horse's Tale." We have six members. Mrs. Smith, Mrs. Hoyt and Mrs. Haley will pick out their book next week. Some of them can afford to buy their books at the bookstore. Mrs. J. Miller has a good selection.

Nov. 3, 1907

I have been elected the treasurer of the W.C.T.U. I have belonged since we ministered in Cushing. The latest newspaper had a long article about the danger of having heavier than air machines flying over our heads. When they have problems they just tumble down on whatever is under them. I will never ride in one.

We had our get-together of the Book Club and we had a great time telling the others about the book we had read.

Nov. 14, 1907

I do not understand but the newspapers have been saying that the USA suffered a financial disaster. Here in Hartland life goes on just as it has for many years. And I cannot understand all the labor strife. Most of the people in Linn Mill are very happy and none of their children go hungry.

Nov. 16, 1907

Well – Dolly proved that when the trains come into town with monsters tooting and tooting even well-trained horses get excited. She reared up and kicked the wagon so hard that James will need more than a few dollars to get it repaired. He had gone to get the District Superintendent who is holding the Church's Quarterly conference tomorrow. Rev. Henry Warren will be staying with us.

Nov. 21, 1907

Mrs. Haley, the lawyer's wife, had a most instructive report on Upton Sinclair's novel "The Jungle."

Dec. 5, 1907

I have a Christmas pageant and the girls and boys have read it once. Will start practicing Saturday.

Dec. 20, 1907

The young people are going to make us proud. They sing on key and louder than any other group I have coached. I am going to make sure that James visits their parents and gives them a special invite. James please say, "Come and be proud of your son or daughter."

Dec. 28, 1907

We had a large congregation for both the morning service and the evening one where the young people did an outstanding job. It gives one such a warm feeling when the story of Jesus is so well presented. I am sure that some in the audience were moved to accept Jesus as their savior. We got a letter from James' brother Sam. He is in North Carolina. A letter also from Mother with news of family. Ten-year-old Rupert, Courtney's pride, broke a leg falling out a hay loft. Mother says Courtney keeps her house well stocked with food and firewood. She helps tend his boys when needed. We had Miss Linn for another meal and found that her father had once planned to go to Port Elgin to visit the woolen mills there. She thought her father might have wanted to import some of the woolen cloth from Port Elgin.

This town has good people. Most every one is trustworthy and works for his bread. We have no paupers nor a poor farm.

Jan. 3, 1908

The D.S., when he was with us, said that we will be here for another year. That is good. I am not getting much better but a move always seems to upset my health somewhat. Now we have made good progress in filling the pews in this Grace Linn M.E. Church. We took the train to Bangor. Fred P. was at Bangor First and he had asked us to come and visit. We did visit them but stayed at the Bangor House as I sometimes leak blood and that would not do at all on your hosts' sheets.

Fred had an evening for us to meet several of the local pastors at his home. Before we left we both shopped for some clothing. I got a blue hat and a suit to match, some stockings and underwear. James got about the same as he always does. The same hat and the same shirts.

Feb. 2, 1908

The newspaper came today. Labor problems and financial. I am glad that James has a steady income. It is not large but $900 per year will keep us clothed and fed. We women have had so much enjoyment with our Book Club. Miss Linn has joined us and she adds a more professional touch to our meetings.

Mar. 3, 1908

Now the wind and snow came and made James stay home for four days. I read to James from the latest book that I am going to report to our Club. We then had a discussion about the ideas presented.

Aunt May Dobson

Uncle David Dobson

There is no entertainer like the Victor

Whether a few friends stop in, or you invite a whole house full of company, or whether you are all alone in the evening, the **Victor** is just the entertainer you need.

It brings to you the magnificent voices of the greatest operatic stars, the stirring music of celebrated bands and orchestras, the liveliest dance music, solos and duets on your favorite instrument, beautiful sacred music, the latest song hits, ministrel shows – the best entertainment of every kind by the world's best talent.

Why not come in and hear this wonderful musical instrument? Find out for yourself what a great entertainer it is. We'll gladly play any Victor music you want to hear.

You can get a Victor for as little as $10. Other styles from $17.50 to $250. Easy terms if desired.

March 31, 1908

Another birthday. I am 36 and James got me another blue diary. He did not say where he bought it nor what it cost. We are still not so old for he kissed me with passion and we ended up in the bed very early that night.

April 10, 1908

We got a letter some time back that the East Maine Conference would be held in Houlton. They have built a new church building. We will go to Bangor and stay overnight at the Bangor House again – I love it!

April 14, 1908

We ate the evening meal with James Watson from Boothbay, Charles Smith of Rockport and Rev. Harry Hoyt of Wiscasset. Then we took the night train to Houlton.

April 15, 1908

As is our custom we gave our testimonials at Houlton and helped in all the ways we were asked. Bishop John Hamilton had a very vigorous message. We were all enthused and full of eagerness in our work in bringing Christ to the unsaved.

April 25, 1908

Candy had the back stoop covered with mice and a few rats when we came home from the Conference. That is what is good about cats. They can fend for themselves. She hunts the whole neighborhood. James will visit all the families that are within driving distance. That is about five miles at the most. Dolly has been behaving better about the train. James says she is almost as smart as Maud.

May 24, 1908

We have several new members and that is good for we also lost a number to sickness. Just three due to accidents,

one in the mill, one in the forest and one on the trains.
Many had been long-time members of the church. We
have had some young people lost in boating mishaps.
That is the saddest funeral service that James has had to
preach.

June 12, 1908

I will ask if there are a few young girls that want to
gather wild food, mushrooms and berries. As I have done
before, I will have Bible study before having classes in
sewing. Then a botany class and then field trips. Wild
food is God's free gift to man. I will continue my Book
Club – it is most informative.

July 10, 1908

As is the custom, a big parade on the 4th of July.
Today my botany girls are going to prepare a full meal
from the bounty of the forest and field. From fiddleheads
to wild onions all cooked with tasty mushrooms. I would
ask James to join but he has stomach problems that do
not like to be aggravated. Most of the girls have brothers
and sisters and I suggested that they teach them about
God's free food. We had a tasty supper with hot biscuits
and good butter.

August 20, 1908

The DS was here and he talked a lot about the forest
fires. Maine needs to save its trees for they are the
livelihood of many of the common people. The notion of
building lookouts on high places was brought up and we
all agreed that it certainly would help keep the fires
smaller.

Sept. 20, 1908

The sun was covered with smoke for the last few
days. Must be a forest fire???

DIARY

1908 – 1913

Sept. 27, 1908

Some of the church men went hunting a few days ago and have come back with quite a few deer. They brought us the hind quarter. After I had cut some of the steaks, I cut the rest into small pieces suitable for canning. I will make a hearty soup from them this winter. I sent a letter to Stella and asked if they would like to come to Hartland for Thanksgiving. I do hope they can.

Oct. 15, 1908

The D.S. came and is spending the night with us. He said the Bishop was considering sending us, no James, to Caribou. I told him that the people there were very friendly when we went there for the East Maine conference of 1902. Rev. Fred Palladino had told us more than once how much he liked serving in Aroostook. We all remembered that Rev. Palladino had Evangelist Gale and Hatch from the United Evangelistic Services.

Nov. 28, 1908

Stella and Bob came for Thanksgiving. We had a great time eating and reminiscing. They have been getting along great after Mrs. Hodgdon died. Bob redid most of the old house. He said he was not sorry that he sold the new one he had built. He came with clams, fish, and several lobsters. Bob did the cooking of the clams and lobsters. They were just a delight to have for a few days. Yet, I know that Stella will take over the running of your house if she stays too long. As she did once.

Dec. 29, 1908

We had the usual good Christmas activity. There is a difference. These boys and girls could not keep on the notes. They were loud and good in trying to do as you directed. Well, not everyone is the Swedish nightingale or the famous Maine opera singer.

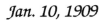

Jan. 10, 1909

The newspaper had a big advertisement about Mr. Ford's new model T. They say the average worker in the car factory can afford to buy one. But most of the roads here would be covered with snow half of the year and mud at least a third of a year. We will not buy one but some foolish people soon will. And the doctors will have more bones to set. The Wright brothers have been trying to sell their flying machine to the U.S. government. I cannot imagine why?

March 12, 1909

The Americans have changed the most useful coin, the Indian head penny, to the head of one of their truly great Presidents, Abraham Lincoln. The whole world honors that man and God himself, as the Irish are wont to say, will applaud Abe Lincoln when he enters heaven.

March 24, 1909

Bishop Luther Wilson was most gratifying in his speech at Bucksport. We spent three days at the Conference. I enjoyed seeing the Charlies again. David Tribou is the secretary for Eastern Maine.

March 26, 1909

Yesterday and last night the wind blew a gale and the snow piled up in mammoth drifts.

March 31, 1909

Another birthday. I am 37. It was just us two. We had some popcorn and did some reading.

April 2, 1909

We are not packing for Caribou. Bishop changed his mind. We are to stay in Hartland.

April 10, 1909

I read in the paper today about how cold this winter has been. It was really cold in Caribou. There was a long article about the ice in Belfast harbor. They reported that Belfast harbor was ice-bound for several months. Much longer than the usual two or three days. The ice cleared April 4, and the needed coal and other things came into the port.

July 4, 1909

The Epworth league marched in the 4th parade. I watched from the sidelines. It was quite an impressive show. There are many veterans of the Civil War who came and marched in force.

Aug. 26, 1909

I have been in bed sick with mostly the same problem. Dr. Moulton came by most every day. James had to hire Mrs. Sweet, an elderly lady. She fed James and kept the house clean. She also helped me in many ways. Dr. Moulton confided in me one day that I would probably not get over this illness – completely.

Sept. 10, 1909

James hired a young girl to help me with running the house. Pearl Higgins comes from a good family but I think her mother kept her from doing household tasks. In one week then I told her that I was not going to teach her how to take care of a house. She did not do a thing well or even good.

Oct. 7, 1909

I have a great lady, Mrs. Claire Johnston, to help take care of the house. She cleans, bakes, washes and is good company for me. We get along nicely. She is a widow and has two sons away which frequently send her money. But my dollars will help her if something should happen to those sons. She is keeping some in the bank.

Nov. 30, 1909

Robert Perry got to the North Pole – so the newspapers are reporting. I wonder how one would know if he was there. Mother wrote me a long letter and it sort of made me homesick. So right after Thanksgiving I said to James, "It has been a very long, long time James dear – too long a time since I have seen my family in Port Elgin. If we went by Pullman I am sure I can make it. Can we go?" And DEAR James went and made the arrangements the very next day.

Dec. 12, 1909

Now we are in Port Elgin staying at Mother's. We left on the train right after church last week. We got to Port Elgin on Tuesday and we will leave Saturday.

Dec. 13, 1909

Wednesday we all went to visit Courtney as he has a big house. We met some of the family for the first time. The children were well-behaved. Eldora had a helper and she did have a great supper. Mother, James and I, Eldora and Courtney, Reta and Avery Oulton, Ernest and Minnie – all nine of us sat around the big table in the dining room. The children had a table in the kitchen. We had brought presents for them all – so after we had sung some good church songs we gave them presents.

Dec. 14, 1909

A few of our friends came to Mother's house the next day for a visit.

Dec. 18, 1909

Now we are home in Hartland, and Mrs. Johnston has the house shining and food ready to eat. I went to bed as soon as I had finished my supper. The train ride was long and I did not sleep well in the Pullman.

Dec. 25, 1909

We have had a snowstorm overnight that will keep the trains from running and most of the people of Hartland in their homes. Maine has storms and this one was a mighty one. Praise God that we were not on our way home from visiting Mother.

Jan. 1, 1910

A new year here in Hartland. I have decided that I must get up and do some work for the Lord even when it pains me. And so I have taken some of the teaching work for the Sunday School.

March 12, 1910

Conference will be at Calais, Maine this year.

April 29, 1910

We have been to Calais the 25th-29th. It was a very long trip but I am glad I went. James was made asst. tres. for the conference. We did get to eat with our friends, the Charleses and Fred P. David Tribou had breakfast with us. Bishop William Qualey did a great service to the conference. He made a very good presentation on the folly of not joining with the Maine conference. As always the singing was very uplifting and the pipe organ was in very good hands and it responded.

May 1, 1910

We are packing to go to Caribou.

May 9, 1910

We have been in Caribou for a few days. On the train coming north we saw snow piled over the telegraph lines. I wonder how they kept the track open? This morning the sun is shining and the snow has gone almost overnight. Spring is finally here. I was afraid it had forgotten to return. But my God sustained me throughout those long, cold, dark days. Now I will give thanks to my God for I know the grass will be green and sun will warm me as He does my soul.

May 13, 1910

I have joined the G.A.R. I have found that many members have no church. I will lead them to know HIM.

May 20, 1910

I was remiss in keeping my diary, well just a bit too much under the weather. So I failed to keep the diary concerning our coming to Caribou – so I will now tell it in a story form:

GOING NORTH

After the Bishop had told James of his next church, we soon gathered our belongings (more now) and took the early train from Bangor. We had our noon meal on the train. When we were seated there was a priest who was still waiting for a table. They were all full. We had room and so James got up and asked the man if he wished to join us. He did and we were amazed for he was Father Joseph Hogan going to Holy Rosary Church in Caribou. The more we conversed with him, the more I heard the new Irish of Amherst. Then Boston came up in our conversation and this Joseph Hogan had lived there in his teenage years. His home was close to Hyde Park. He sure had the breath of Ireland on him.

Mostly woods and not till we got to Houlton was there many fields.

We had supper with Joseph and talked until we came into Caribou. It has grown since we were here in 1902. When we arrived at the station, several Methodist leaders *(Added later in pencil, they were Misters T.D. Little, F.M. Poland and F.E. Hale)* were there to help us move to the parsonage.

The building was big and our furniture fit it nicely and got lost in the large rooms. But I had to hire two young girls to help me clean. One was a young Miss Turner, she would only take half her pay.

June 6, 1910

James came home for a noonday meal and said he had accidentally read about the 25th of April's meeting. James said, and he quoted, "The majority of the members of the official board, after a careful consideration, do not approve of a change of Pastors in Caribou and request the return of Bro. Edmund." James said it was sent as a telegram to the Bishop. "James," I said, "I believe the Lord has sent you to Caribou and James we can give our testimony every day. They will come to love you as I have."

James then said, "Well, they have me and I now know why the Bishop sent me here – these Methodists need to build a new larger church and I will help them build it with God's help and yours, Bessie."

We have a great number of dedicated members and I know that with prayer and hard work by us we will be able to do both the Bishop's plan and God's here in Caribou.

June 15, 1910

Last night we had for Sunday dinner not chicken nor beef or pork. Yes, we had a salmon from the Aroostook river. One of Mrs. Floyd Sweet's sons, James, gave it to me on Saturday. Now freshwater fish hasn't the flavor of saltwater fish, but it was nice and mild. I made an egg sauce to put over it. James said it went very good with the wild cranberry jelly (a gift from Viona Sousis) and boiled potatoes (from Sara Washburn). Salted cod was the staple at home and it is in Caribou. I do feel at home here and am more able to do God's work in this community than that of Boston. That was a strange time in mine and James' life. He studied. I walked and cooked and didn't feel at home in Hyde Park. Yet God was there, I know, but his work in that strange land I didn't or could not do as well as I had hoped. I am praising God and am ever so thankful that we are serving Him here.

July 4, 1910

Bands played and we had a parade. I marched with the G.A.R. and we had a grand supper at the hall. Joe Hogan came and we had a good talk. He gave the blessing. I wonder how some of his French members understand him. His Irish brogue is very heavy. The people like him very much as a person.

July 24, 1910

We have had given to us by the people of Caribou, strawberries, meat, fish, potatoes, bread and oh yes, those tangy fiddleheads. They have come from Alice Griffin, Bertha Powers, Viola Sousis, Sarah Harmon, Sarah Washburn, Sarah Smith and Mary Brown. That is all I can think of now.

Aug. 2, 1910

I bought the Ladies Home Journal for 15 cents and read the article titled "The Men we Love and the Men we Marry." Just about every woman in town was talking about it so I had to read it. If we had a Book Club I would have given a report already.

Dec. 10, 1910

My! Such a large number of high-school-age children. I will have to scramble to find the right Christmas play to include them all. This church is bursting its seams. We can hardly all squeeze in every Sunday. The leaders are considering a new one. This was a year that the politicians finally put limits on how long women and children could work. 58 hours per week and the children were to be 16.

Jan. 1, 1911

Good news! The sheriff of the county, Elmer Brayson, said that he will enforce the prohibition laws in Aroostook. We have plans to have brother Rev. Ora Samuel and J.J. Lowe for evangelistic meetings this winter. James has had a letter saying that they would soon let him know if they could come.

Jan. 4, 1911

We now know where James' brother has been. He wrote and told us about the Evangelist organization that he is with. A Rev. Gale is the organizer. They offered to send Brother Samuel and Rev. J.J. Lowe to preach for a week.

Jan. 10, 1911

The official Broad on Sunday, James said, that Misters Ebbett, Lyons, Smith, Varnum, Sraight, Hight, Gray, Mary Campbell, Mrs. Pollard, Mr. Poland met in the church vestry and authorized him to rent the opera house for a week for the evangelistic meetings.

Jan. 12, 1911

Ora Samuel Gray, James' older brother, and Lowe sent a telegram saying they will come for a week. James had rented the Opera house for that time. Miss Gretchen Ebbett (16 years at that time and to become Mrs. Amos Fletcher Sr.) and her mother Mrs. Gretchen Ebbett volunteered to play the piano.

Jan. 31, 1911

The Opera House was full every night and many new people are now coming to the Baptist and the Free Baptist and our Methodist Church. Joe Hogan came by for supper at my pleading. He is so nice to have around. A great gentleman. He said that even if his church did not take part, the results were that more of his people came to church more often.

Feb. 3, 1911

The ladies of the Episcopal Church did a play on the Longfellow poem about Hiawatha. We went and enjoyed their company.

March 31, 1911

I had the Ladies Aid of the church here for the afternoon for Tea and some nice cookies. My birthday. We took time to read from the Bible. And we had Dr. Trustee tell how best to keep from catching tuberculosis. That disease seems to kill our young people when they offer the world so much.

April 2, 1911

The official Board took under advisement that the present church building is no longer large enough for the growing congregation.

April 16, 1911

We are at the Bangor House. It is as nice a place as it was before. We came down from Caribou in a Pullman car. We left on the evening train right after an afternoon Sunday School in Woodland. It is nice to be treated to the luxury of sleeping as you travel. Sleeping in the nicest white sheets and under warm clean blankets. Breakfast was served on a white tablecloth and we passed on our usual oatmeal and had ham and eggs, toast with just wonderful coffee. I could get to really enjoy being waited on like that. They all were Negroes and they said, "Good Morn' Ma'm, and Sir right t'is way," and they pulled out the chair for me.

I need to tell, that I, well, we would have taken the coach but for a nice Mr. Poland. He came and said to James dear, "Now you take these two tickets I bought for you and Bessie. We know that she is willing to ride the coach but she has been off her feed for some time now, so Reverend, take them and don't bother with the thanks. My wife and I can part with that sum for my Lord Jesus Christ – Yes Sir." I am going to send them a thank you note as soon as I can.

We took the new electric cars to the Methodist church for our annual conference in Old Town. We are not ready for automobiles.

April 17, 1911

The Eastern Maine Conference is being held in Old Town under Bishop Earl Cranston. It is well attended. James and I both gave our testimonials. Our friend Fred P. was appointed to First Methodist in Bangor. Charles Smith had breakfast with us each morning. James has been making speeches about the joining of the two conferences in Maine. James is all for it. Now we have railroads to take us quickly anywhere in the state – why shouldn't we all be together.

April 18, 1911

What a delight it is to sing and pray with so many devout fellow workers in our Lord's Garden. We meet so many old friends and then we make new ones which we will see next conference. The Bishop is a powerful speaker and his message fills my soul. He makes me want to do more and more with James to bring more people into the fold – Jesus' fold. We Methodists need to do a better job of telling of the love of our Savior Jesus Christ.

April 19, 1911

We are going to return to Caribou and James is now planning on a new large church building. James is sure that it is God's plan to build a suitable church for the three hundred souls that will worship at the new Peoples Methodist Episcopal church in our growing town in Aroostook. Lord, I love the people and I love to give my testimonial to our Congregation. May my health improve, the pain go away so that I can do the Lord's work for many years.

April 25, 1911

On the train coming home we slept late but when we awoke the sun was shining. I pained all night but breakfast with James was a blessing. We put together a list of those people who had the best ability to do the various jobs which would make the new church a reality. We had supper at home and James is in bed. I'll soon join him. Got to put out Candy the cat.

May 2, 1911

The Bangor paper came today with the most awful news. A fire started in a hay barn and set the whole city aflame. After I got done reading it, I prayed for those who had died and those whose places had gone up in flames.

James come home for supper, and we discussed the possibility of organizing a relief effort for those poor unfortunate people. I am going to get the Methodist Ladies Aid involved and also the Taylor (G.A.R.) men and women. James said John Howes will help and so will James Withee. I said, "James let us get started by having them both come for supper before we have prayer meeting."

May 6, 1911

Automobiles have come to Caribou. E.E. Powers took one off the B & A Railroad and drove it up and down Sweden Street all day. He hopes to sell them here in Aroostook. A few showoffs will buy them. The roads are for horses and wagons. I dare say that most bridges are too.

May 7, 1911

Praise God for these wonderful people of Caribou. They have enthusiasm for filling the Lord's command. A most generous offering was taken and sent to the District Super (name if I can) for him to help those poor needy souls in Bangor. The Taylor Post also sent a large generous donation to the Mayor of Bangor.

May 20, 1911

We had a marriage at the parsonage today. Not a very big affair – seems like there will be a baby soon. They are not members of Peoples Church. They did, however, promise to be Christians and the wife said they would come back to have the baby baptized. I am always ready to forgive people and I pray for them every evening. That happened in Port Elgin and sometime the Church was most cruel to them. I think it better the way James did it. He talked calmly to them about how Jesus would forgive them if they asked for forgiveness. I felt that they were willing to ask for it and it gave them some reasons for becoming church members.

June 3, 1911

The Maine Bible Society came to Caribou and we and the other churches are doing a religious census. I went to see Dr. Little today. He gave a prescription and I got it filled at Havey's.

June 6, 1911

We have been given $10,000 by Andrew Carnegie for a library. Now the library trustees and the town are having a terrible time over the place to build it. I hope that it will be a large enough lot so that someday in the distant future the building can be expanded.

June 10, 1911

We have a new project at Sunday School. My dear young ladies made the decision that they would like to help the town with the Library. So they will bring their pennies for six months. Mona Davis said that they could help the ladies of the church when they had ice cream sales. All twenty of the young girls are most enthusiastic about the coming library. The town is very grateful to Mr. Carnegie for his contribution. I am very glad and said to them that they must thank God for all the blessings that will happen over the many, many years that the Library will serve the town of Caribou. We just might have a Book Club like we had in Hartland.

June 11, 1911

Today was our first meeting on the Sweden Road. I led them in songs, read the Bible and took up a small collection of 45 pennies. We had 39 out of the 40 that had said they would come. They were well-behaved and I am so happy that I can help my dear James and lead the young girls and boys into the Christian fold. I did this as soon as we had our lunch after church. We got one of the older girls to carry some helpers in her wagon. I can take four in mine. James has to have a sermon ready for the Sunday evening. He needs time to think and be led by the Spirit. I am blessed with such a good man and the joy to have him to work beside.

June 12, 1911

My dear James has finally organized forty young children on the New Sweden Road in the Woodland village. They are going to meet in the school. I am going to be the leader with help from some of our young high school girls – two of the Vinals girls and Jane Dupont and her sister, said they would help. I plan to make four classes using the corners of the room. I hope to have two young ladies per class. I'll conduct the joint session. I thank God for this work to do in his vineyard. We will do this each Sunday afternoon while James will be doing a service at the Lyndon school building at Lyndon Center. On the outskirts of this town are many young people who need a chance to attend church.

June 23, 1911 – The Funeral

Corydon Powers' funeral today at the church. The church was on the point of bursting its walls. Truly not one more person could have entered. The Rev. Charles

McEthiney came up from Searsport. He was a former pastor. Dr. Tuell, Ray Ebbett, A.W. Spaulding and Ray Brown sang beautifully. There was sixty men from the Caribou Lodge, 170 F and Am. They were joined by the G.A.R. and the Caribou Grange. I led the Women's Relief Corps into the sanctuary. Corydon was a farmer and well-liked Republican legislator. The community will miss his goodness and the Caribou Methodist church will miss this fervent supporter.

Corydon has two sons, Elmer and Delbert, twins I think. Two daughters – one is married to Olaf Pierson. Bertha has been seeing the Spaulding boy.

July 4, 1911

Caribou had their 4th of July parade on the hottest day I have ever lived through. The newspaper said most of New England had temperatures into the 100s. I did not take part.

July 10, 1911

Every Sunday the church is more than full. This building was very good when the congregation numbered around a hundred and fifty but we are much more than that now. And more come every Sunday! It is still nearly 100 degrees here in northern Maine. What must it be like in Hyde Park?

Aug. 10, 1911

Most of the Church leaders agree that a new church is needed. But money is not easily found. Yet James is saying to them most every Sunday, "Put your faith in God and pray that this congregation called The Peoples Methodist Episcopal Church in Caribou will find that it can build a suitable church building to the Glory of God."

It is needed yet still most folks ask where we can find the money.

Aug. 21, 1911

We have electric lights and a telephone and I have heard that signals are now going through the air in almost instant time. We got the results today of the religious census. The total number of families in Caribou was 1196. Methodist 173, Free Baptist 155, Baptist 155, Catholics 315, Universalist 81, and NO CHURCH 371. James is most anxious to reach those with no church connection.

Sept. 12, 1911

We had the Rev. and Mrs. Ferguson, Baptist, for an evening meal. The Unitarian, Rev. Blair, left before we got to meet him. I served roast pork, sweet potatoes, carrots and my canned peas. For bread I had yeast-risen rolls. We had cake and ice cream for dessert with coffee. They had read "Black Beauty." I had but James never has that much time. We sang and got to know each other.

Sept. 17, 1911

It has been very cold now and the farmers are afraid that some potatoes will get frosted and spoil in their potato houses.

Sept. 18, 1911

The Aroostook County sheriff and the town fathers are going to enforce prohibition. I hope they do. The W.C.T.U. in Caribou is very active. I joined as soon as I could. Yes, a long time ago.

Oct. 30, 1911

That horse, Hazard, James bought from Livi Gary tipped the wagon over and dear James was crushed against a large rock that seriously injured his back and right leg. Mrs. Lyons and I received small cuts and bruises. James had driven from Lyndon Center to pick us up. We were in Woodland and had finished the Sunday

School service and were ready to leave. Something, I know not what, caused Hazard to rear up and he swung to the right so quick and forcefully that we were all dumped onto the ground. Mrs. Lyons and I were cut and bleeding, but poor dear James hit a large sharp rock which hurt his left leg very badly and he also injured his back. Two church women who had seen the accident turned their wagons back and with Mrs. Lyons and I we got James back into the wagon after we had righted it. James was only able to tell us how to do that.

Dr. Edgar W. Sincock came by at my request, upon our arriving home. He said John had no broken bones. For which I am grateful. He recommended a mustard plaster which I started using that very night.

Sunday evening at Peoples church James stood up the whole service, but it took big Ezekiel Gonier and wiry Nathan Lufkin to help me put dear James to bed.

Nov. 10, 1911

Today dear James felt like hitching Hazard to the wagon and doing his visitation. He still limps a little. I drove for him and Hazard behaved himself even when one of those automobiles went racing by us and threw up a large cloud of dust. I'll have to wash our things. We best wear old coats until they put their autos up for the winter. I like to travel by train and at times by a wagon but I hope James will never buy an automobile. They make me shiver in fright every time I see one racing down the road. I do not wish ever to ride in one. Today had a sharp pain in my bowels that lasted until I took one of those pills Dr. Sincock gave me. I have had pains before, but never so long and sharp.

Nov. 23, 1911

It is Thanksgiving here in the U.S.. In Canada it is the second Monday in October. We had C.E. Johnson and his friend Bud Wood to share our Thanksgiving dinner. They entertained us with local stories.

Dec. 10, 1911

We found out from John Lyons after he had come back from Washburn on the electric line that Percy Dow had moved into the Washburn parsonage from Presque Isle to be the new Minister for the M.E. church. James will visit with him soon. The D.S. in Bangor asked James to give Percy whatever help he might need.

Dec. 20, 1911

I am sure the official board will give the go-ahead for the building of a new Church. They had a very long meeting on Dec. 18 and James said he was almost certain that at their next meeting they would authorize the buying of the Erving lot. And that the A.J. Goud residence and lot were available at favorable terms. They had already sold the old parsonage to Hight and Page for $3500 and the church building for $6000 to Farrell and Berce.

Dec. 30, 1911

They have hired the Architects and Builders, Astle and Page, and appointed building committee – C.E. Varnum, H.W. Ebbett, O.D. Smith, and P.N. Hight. Finance just the right men, F.M. Pollard, P.N. Hight and James.

Dec. 31, 1911

More Marriage – The Smiths, Jacob Smith's daughter Bessie was joined together with Floyd Smith by my dear James at the Peoples Church at seven this evening. We had Smiths and more Smiths from far and wide. A very good reception after at the church. We will be having Smiths in the congregation.

Jan. 1, 1912

Winter in Caribou is colder than any place we have ever been. The snow crunches when you step on it and the house makes dreadful noises as it contracts. We have piles and piles of snow. I wait for the sunny days to go buy food.

March 26, 1912

I hired that Turner girl for a few days. Celia asked Mrs. Hussey for a few days off to help me out. I wanted to make the parsonage house shine. I was planning a birthday – mine – so we could invite some people that are not Methodist.

April 1, 1912

So yesterday we had sixteen people come for an evening of fun and food. We had to use the kitchen table and all of our dishes. Celia Turner came and helped serve the food. She brought a younger sister, Sadie, to wash the dishes. We had a great time singing and no one got into any religious arguments even though we were of many persuasions.

April 3, 1912

The Conference in Rockland with Bishop William Bart was the fastest moving one we have ever had. He must have had another conference to go to very soon. We had barely time to say hello to our friends called Charles, Smith, Jones and dear David Tribou. We had a meal with Fred P.   James was elected as a trustee. James is going to have $1600 per year. We had time to spend two nights, one going and one coming, at the Bangor House.

August 23, 1912

The local paper had a story about an Indian, Andrew Sockalexis, from Maine in a marathon in Sweden. He came fourth. Woodrow Wilson is running for President.

Sept. 9, 1912

We did not go the Fair in Presque Isle. I was pretty sick most of that week. On Tuesday it thundered and rain came down in buckets. The rain collected and water ran down the potato rows and washed out some fields. Wednesday the sun came out and it was a great fall day. Mary Shaw came by and told me that over 22,000 people came to the fair and they counted over 500 automobiles passing the gate. Mary has a brother who is on the governing board of the fair. The Caribou chief of police said in the paper that he would arrest any person who drove in the town over 20 m.p.h. I hope he means it for they drive out by the church at dangerous rates of speed and there are a lot of men working on our new church. George V. Brown sure has the ability to do a great Sunday school So well organized!

I'm not sure that I like the fact that another movie hall is opening. P.J. Powers has just finished a big building on Sweden Street.

Dr. Cary died in August and left the town quite a large sum of money. Mary Shaw said it would be over a hundred thousand – my what a large sum to save.

Oct. 11, 1912

Old Amos Kelley died the 29th of September. He was a Civil War veteran. Most veterans that are on pension are sent $6 per month. The G.A.R. surely will try to get it increased. They have a big board outside the hardware store and by telegram they are posting the world series between the New York and Boston teams. The world will not be changed by either team winning. I think it is totally unimportant.

I don't complain much but eight cents for milk to be delivered to your door seems a bit too much. In Port Elgin we paid 4 cents and there was more cream in it.

Nov. 13, 1912

My, the farmers are doing well. The paper had a long article about Ralph Pitcher. He said that even if the farmers had to pay high wages for their help and exorbitant prices for fertilizer and machinery yet they still

could build nice new homes and barns, like Howard
Nichols' barn that everybody is talking about. James and I
will have to go see it. I see in the paper that potatoes are
selling good. Woodrow Wilson is the new President.

The D.S. Teagues are moving to California – many
others have gone. I am having bad stabbing pains again.
Old Doctor Cary had given me some Tonic before he died,
but it did not help! I need to see a better doctor – I will
soon.

Nov. 16, 1912

James will have a difficult funeral. Old Mrs. Margaret
Irving died at her daughter's home. Margaret's husband,
Robert, died eight years ago. She was a very well-liked
lady of the community. We had the Rev. Frank Kirkpatrick
here for a noon meal last Tuesday. They had called and
said they were coming over from Washburn on the
electric. It is good to get to know them better.

Nov. 20, 1912

The telephone company needs to hire younger women
for night duty. Every one in town is up in arms when they
ring and get no answer. The Union Church is getting a
new pastor – the Rev. Harry Adams Hersey. We will ask
them along with the Ramsdells' of the Baptist Church.

Dec. 28, 1912

The year has gone by much too fast. James and I have
done our best for the Lord. We find the people of Caribou
most willing to go the extra mile when it is needed. We
have the money or we have promises that will make a
very good building for us Methodists to hold our worship
services. I do wish that someone had the money for a pipe
organ like they had in Boothbay. What a beautiful sound
that made when someone with real talent played it. I
played it, but I am not a trained musician.

Jan. 17, 1913

We sold lots and lots of food at Ray Brown's store today. We can turn in a good deal of money to the G.A.R. for our monument. They say the Baptist Church and the Free Baptist are going to join. I have heard of Free Methodists but have never met one. Ralph Pitcher, that very well-off farmer is rumored to have bought the most expensive car made. It has an electric starter, they say. Well he will have to wait awhile to try it out – we have at least three feet of snow.

April 23-28, 1913

We left the 20th on the night sleeper to Bangor. Bought some new clothes. A new blue hat for the conference. Bishop Theodore Henderson greeted us at the Bucksport electric station. We will stay with the Methodist family of John Flood. He is a good church man. James again spent most of the conference discussing how the two Maine conferences could be one. The Bishop was on James' side. We had breakfast at a restaurant, most mornings with David Tribou and Charles Smith. The Bishop said he would send the drawings (blueprints from the headquarters of the Methodist Church) that the Methodist have all ready drawn for new Methodist churches.

May 3, 1913

The town is again talking about a trotting park. I hope they build it soon for racing horses on Sunday is one of my pet peeves. It might be near Teague Park. I visited Dr. Sincock at James' request and he said that his new pills might just take care of my pain. I do hope so.

Bishop Hamilton has written James and promised to come for the dedication of the new church. The trustees, with Astle and Page, had his plans and they adjusted them to fit the needs of the Peoples Church. We expect that to happen the first of November. I wish my pain

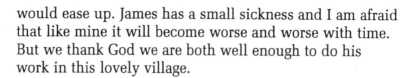

would ease up. James has a small sickness and I am afraid that like mine it will become worse and worse with time. But we thank God we are both well enough to do his work in this lovely village.

May 20, 1913

They have moved the A.V. Goud house. We had to leave and stayed at the Vaughan House. We have eaten there and now we have stayed overnight for a few days. The cement must dry and harden before they set the house on the foundation .As soon as the house was moved the men came with many teams of horses and soon the church basement was excavated.

May 30, 1913

My James has been very busy visiting everyone in our membership. He is telling them that the Church needs their prayers, their presence and gifts. Many stopped coming when we had to rent the Opera House until we have our own building finished.

June 5, 1913

I was at a meeting of the Ladies Relief Corps when a Mrs. Bouchard came and sat next to me. She said, "Mrs. Gray, I have admired the way you Methodists raise money. You have had ice cream socials, bake sales and just about everything but a ploy supper." "What is that?" I exclaimed. She told me what they were and my response was, "That is an idea I could help bring about." Then I asked her, "Mrs. Bouchard will you come and supervise the making of the ploys?"

June 10, 1913

Saturday night we had the biggest ploy supper ever held in Caribou, Mrs. Bouchard and ten of her good friends that had cooked many a ploy. We fed over three hundred people and with their donation of the buckwheat

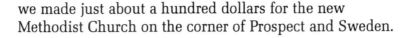

we made just about a hundred dollars for the new
Methodist Church on the corner of Prospect and Sweden.

July 4, 1913

I never stop marveling about this holiday the
Americans make so much of. Canada did not have such a
day where all the veterans march with bands and school
kids of many stripes. I did not join the G.A.R. in marching
as my bowels have been most painful of late. I am going
to see Dr. Little.

Aug. 12, 1913

It seems that the frame of the Church is nearly up.
They hope to finish the work soon. We have continued to
have fewer people at our services. We need a church
building. The inside of a church is conducive to worship
as compared to a theater.

Aug. 17, 1913

Some of the glorious new stained glass windows have
been put in – others are coming. The paper says that
some men are interested in having a trotting park over by
Teague. That would stop those Sunday races by our town
churches. We had a supper at the P. of H. hall and made a
lot of money for the monument project. I work at all of
these doings even when I pain quite badly. I think it is my
duty to the community as Christ would have me do. So
I'll spend a day in bed. It will put me back on my feet.

Oct. 1, 1913

I sent the new meeting times to the paper for dear
James. He has so many things to do with the Bishop
coming and the finishing of our beautiful new church.
The meeting times will be, I'm writing them here as they
have changed from the old church where we tried to
avoid worship when the horsemen were racing.

10:30 Public Worship 3:00 Jr. League
12:00 Sunday School 7:00 Evening Service
At the New Peoples Methodist Episcopal Church. We are so proud and happy.

Nov. 2, 1913

Sunday Morning and we have standing room only. The Bishop is here to dedicate this Church building. The L.O.L. organization were guests at the first service in our new church and were in full uniform. We had evangelist services in the evening.

Nov. 3, 1913

The Rev. W.F. Davis, D.D. of Houlton preached a great evangelistic service at 7:30 Monday evening.

Nov. 8, 1913

We had our Peoples Quarterly Conference at which the Bishop stressed his gratitude that we paid off our debt before the dedication.

Nov. 9, 1913

We had at 9:30 the Sacrament of the Lord's Supper to a full house. Rev. A.E. Morris, Superintendent of Bangor District, preached at 10:30. That evening the W.C.T.U. had charge of the service.

Nov. 10, 1913

Rev. G.F. Durgin, Vice President of the East Maine Conference Seminary gave an address at 7:30 at our church. The Northern Bangor District Association held all day meetings – Nov. 11, 12, 13, 14 and 15, in our NEW church building.

Nov. 16, 1913

Sunday – Finally Bishop John Hamilton dedicated the debt free Caribou's Peoples Methodist Church at the 10:30

service. Then Sunday afternoon at 2:30 we had short addresses by the Bishop, Rev. A.E. Morris and local Pastors. At 7:30 the church was filled with special music by the Church Choir.

Nov. 21, 1913

The wedding of the year – no such wedding for the next twenty or so years. Nearly half the town was at the Powers home. Too bad that Corydon had not lived to see his beautiful young daughter, Bertha Leola, marry Atwood William Spaulding. That family nearly spoiled their son Atwood for they gave him around the world trip for his graduating present!! But he is a smart young man, he was on Governor Powers (Houlton) staff. They really did the house up in yellow chrysanthemums from Harold Chadwick's place in Houlton. He and two of our young ladies, Avis Washburn and Edna Knowles, furnished the music. The bride was lovely, attired in cream-colored brocaded chiffon. The ceremony was performed by Rev. Harvey Adams Hersey (Unitarian) and my dear James. President Todd of B and A Railroad sent his private car up to Caribou to speed them on their honeymoon in Jamaica.

Dec. 2, 1913

The young Albert Belyea who was here in Aug. and did such a good job of preaching at the church and at Woodland is back in town and James said I should call and have him come to supper. James and I are both trying to be helpful to any young man who wants to do the work of the Lord. He has been attending the Weslyan Seminary. The Aroostook Tel and Tel has got their operators to stay awake during the night AND answer the customers' calls.

The Free Baptists over in Fort Fairfield have a minister, Rev. W.E. Kirkpatrick, according to the paper. I wonder if he is related to Frank?

Dec. 3, 1913

Once again a Christmas pageant has to be performed. And this year in the Opera House. Well, a stage will have some advantages. Now I need to find the right play to fit the talent of my girls. I will get help from the boys' leader of The Epworth League, Ray Ebbett.

Dec. 20, 1913

A brand new brick building for the Aroostook Trust. It is most imposing and very well done. Mr. King is the President.

Jan. 1, 1914

This house has a big furnace and a lovely fireplace and we can afford coal and wood and stay warm even when the north wind howls and screams all night. That lovely furnace keeps us warm.

Feb. 10, 1914

The movies are here to stay – some are worth seeing. The librarian and I saw the Perils of Pauline. I am not sure young people should see this movie, it would frighten them way too much.

PACKARD
MADE IN AMERICA

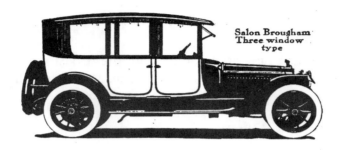

Salon Brougham
Three window
type

Many American buyers of foreign cars have been influenced largely by habit. But invariably their first purchase of a Packard has shown them the superior worth of the American-made car. In large proportion, they have been converted because they have realized in the Packard an expression of their own thought and taste, coupled with the superlative quality in performance on the road.

Ask the man who owns one

PACKARD MOTOR CAR COMPANY
DETROIT

Diary

1914 – 1919

March 31, 1914

Another birthday – I am having a group from the book readers club of the library for my birthday. We will have it in the afternoon and will make popcorn and molasses candy.

April 2, 1914

We all took turns reading from Willa Cather's book "Alexander's Bridge." We read most of the afternoon. She is a very fine writer. The paper says the war with Mexico is over.

April 15-21, 1914

The conference met in Presque Isle. They have a new church building. John Hamilton, the Bishop, is an old friend now. Some of the appointments for Aroostook were friend Ed Allen to Presque Isle and Mapleton, Frank Kirkpatrick for Washburn. We had supper with David Tribou and Charles Plumber. They came over to our house in Caribou. We bought lunch one day in Presque Isle and ate with Al Luce and Al Morris. Many other friends were there and we all enjoyed the new church building. They have a very good choir. We are going to continue on in Caribou. My old cat Candy was gone when we came home. She may have died someplace. I hope she just fell asleep. Sometimes when I am sick, I think that it is time the Lord called me home. Then I get revived and I am ready to do his work with more determination. The spring is coming and the weather will warm and my spirit and body will again be eager to do my Lord Jesus' commands.

May 23, 1914

The telephone rang and rang. I ran up the cellar stairs to answer it. I panted "Hello" and it was echoed back by a strange voice. Hello I said again, then I heard the voice say, "I am calling for James Gray." Well dear James was over in the church. So I said to the voice, "I'll tell him your message." It was long distance so the man agreed. He was George Stott who was one of the first people we met at our first Methodist conference in Maine. He wanted to tell James that the newly appointed pastor in Presque Isle was to be Edward Allen. George had been their pastor. I thanked him for the news and when James came for supper we decided to have the Allens over for supper soon. We already knew that news. Allen was also a friend we had got to like at our yearly conferences. The Presque Isle church was built by Astel and Page of Houlton the same as who did our Caribou church building. Bishop Hamilton was in Presque Isle for their dedication.

Aug. 5, 1914

The whole town is talking about the war between England and Germany. I can recall that some leader of Canada warned that Germany was getting too big for her britches. He wanted Canada to build its defenses but some small-fry in Quebec was dead opposed.

Aug. 6, 1914

Canada has gone to war with Germany.

Aug. 10, 1914

Young boys and girls have sold us the bounty of nature from fiddleheads, strawberries, blueberries, hazelnuts and soon some apples. Canada is going to send men to fight against the Germans.

Aug. 12, 1914

A short note from mother to say Courtney has another boy his name is Everret. She is well and has had to hire help only rarely.

Sept. 12, 1914

What a year gone so far. I got involved early on with the Ansel G. Taylor Women's Relief Corps #97 G.A.R. (Grand Army of the Republic, Civil War veterans). I was not one to go to town when James and I were in Boston, but I remember the large statue in the park. I was impressed with it. And one night soon after I came to this lovely town I joined the Women's Relief Corps. I think it was a few meetings later that I got talking with Mrs. Fair and told her of that grand monument in Boston. She must have told her husband that very night, and he must have become really enthused about a monument for Caribou. She is inclined to be led by her husband thoughts. At the next meeting she was going around saying to everyone that Caribou should have a soldiers' monument. I talked to James and so we too were soon helping this project along with planning and leading the congregation in building our new church. I have planned many fund raisers for next year for the Monument project.

The author adds: The town of Caribou in 1917 spent $1,000 on the granitic monument and changed the name of the park from Hussey to Monument Park. The statue is in Civil War uniform, but the monument was dedicated to W.W. I veterans. Olley Fair was one of the major players in pushing the citizens of Caribou in their struggles to complete the work of the ladies of the Women's Relief Corps of the G.A.R. Drive by it when you pass the Nylander Museum.

Oct. 2, 1914

The war continues. Canada is sending thousands of men to fight. All of the British Empire have joined England in the war against Germany. Russia has been pushing at the backs of the GERMANS. Trenches are said to go from the North Sea to Switzerland. My history would point out to the English, Lords and King, that this is the first big movement of armed men that is crossing from west to east. I will write Mother about the boys leaving the Port. I am not at all well. I bleed some most every day.

Oct. 5, 1914

The sun is bright off the snow. It was down to -10 degrees in the night and James had to tend the fire twice-- once at parsonage and once at the church. Warm in the kitchen when I made the oatmeal for us. I am thankful for the Smiths that bring us rich cream for our breakfast. Coffee and oats go best with that great taste.

While we ate I had a chance to tell James about the little book I had just finished reading. By a man and wife, Bertha B. and Ernest Cobb. James is so busy that sometimes we hardly get to finish our thoughts as we try to live together. Well he did listen this morning when I explained a bit about their book. The whole story is underlain with a Christian theme. After I had pointed out to dear James that any or all of the Epworth League students would benefit from reading this little book and best of all they could borrow it from the Caribou library, I got up and brought it to show him the music to Arlo's song. Then sang it for him. He joined me and it was lovely as it could be. This story made me more than a little sad at not having a child to bring up. That is one of the blessings we miss. Dear James said he would read the book. I said it would take him only a few hours. James reads rapidly.

Oct. 7, 1914

James finished reading that little book. He said I was right in recommending it for the Epworth students. Then he suggested that the church should buy a few copies. I promised that I would find out where the Library had bought theirs and order five copies. We are having a Ladies Aid meeting today. I am going to give a small talk on why we should all encourage our young people to learn to read and write and some need lessons in music. I think I'll tell them about Arlo's music from the Cobbs'

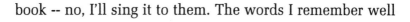

book -- no, I'll sing it to them. The words I remember well
. . .

> "Soft the evening bells are ringing
> Silent shadows fill the sky
> Sweet the birds their vespers singing
> Slumber, slumber, lul-a-bye"

Nov. 2, 1914

The Bishop sent James a long telegram about some problem in a charge that needs to have a new pastor. I am dreading the winter for it seems that as the cold settles in I become less well. I would like to smell the salt air.

Nov. 12, 1914

The Swedes are all mighty proud of one of their own, Olaf Nylander. The paper had a long article about his fossil finds -- I am not quite sure what they are or if they are of any use.

Dec. 1, 1914

The Junior Leaguers have picked out their own play and Mr. G. Brown will take my place this year. I can not commit to such a long time for I might need to go to bed for my health's sake. Yet I plan to help everyone in short term projects if it will be some work that helps the church fulfill its purpose. Letter from Mother saying some twenty left for the Canadian Army.

Dec. 10, 1914

A long phone message to James and also one to the leader of the church. The Rev. Gilbert Edgett, pastor in Rockland, has transferred to The New England Southern Conference. The Bishop is saying that James should come to Rockland and that he will send someone to Caribou soon.

Dec. 20, 1914

The Official Board met and James was give permission to leave and they then thanked him most heartily for the job he had done. We will be leaving for Rockland the very first of January. Charles Plumber is coming to take our place. I have been quite ill.

Mother's letter came with news that Charles Turner, Percy Murray, Isac Gray, two of the Allen boys, and Norton Copp are overseas.

Dec. 27, 1914

George Brown had a great Christmas pageant. What singing and Oh! the readings were given with such conviction. It made me love them all. We are to go to Rockland as soon as we get the furniture packed. My! My! How our collection of chairs and tables has grown. And so many things. I am wishing I had Stella to help do the packing. That will be about the 10th of Jan. I will miss these Caribou people for we have got to know them quite well. And I have loved them.

Jan. 3, 1915

We cried on each others' shoulders and hugged each other that last Sunday in Caribou. Sunday, January 1, will long be remembered. The papers have only bad news about passenger ships being sunk by the Germans.

Jan. 5, 1915

We have been getting ready to go to Bangor. Last night we had the Reverend Joseph Hogan from Holy Rosary here for supper. He is Irish and we both find him a great man at table. He has a book of tales, and they are very good. Most of them with a Christian theme. He sometimes sees better than some of the narrow minded ones. We shall miss him. James informed me today that he thinks Hogan will also be moved.

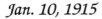

Jan. 10, 1915

All our things are packed and at the B&A. I will miss these people of Caribou. We worked hard in His field and harvested well. Now we will find other fields to cultivate for our Lord. We take the evening train and will sleep in beds all the way there. This modern world has such luxuries. The latest pills from Dr. Sincock have eased my pains somewhat.

As the click clack of train wheels ring in my ears, I write in my diary. We are going to Rockland. I will be near the sea. I am in hopes that the sea air will put me back on my feet. I have been half an invalid all my days in Caribou. Yet I loved the people and as soon as I could gather my strength I did all I could to help James bring more souls to the knowledge of Jesus Christ.

Jan. 11, 1915

Spent the night at the Bangor House and did some clothes buying. We visited the D.S. He could not have a meal with us -- he had a quarterly Conference to go to. Bangor has not completely recovered from that devastating fire. The newspaper was full of war news. We are going on the Maine Central about 10 o'clock in the morning. This reminds me that when we first went to Boston the city had the official time and it was not the same as it was in Hyde Park. Hyde Park was factory oriented and the city of Boston was business oriented. James checked his watch with the desk to be sure we will be there to take the train. When we asked for a cab to the station they asked if we wanted to go in an automobile.

I said, "I will walk first." They called a cab that was horse powered. Bangor is a hustling city and that bustling makes the air full of the stench from those automobiles. Caribou had some but Bangor is overrun with them. They honk and race and honk. I hope that is not what Rockland sounds like.

Jan. 13, 1915

A pleasant ride on the Maine Central Railroad to Rockland. They are so much cleaner and more pleasant than the first one I rode on with James in New Brunswick. I hope Mother writes about my friends that have gone overseas to fight the Germans. The newspaper called them Huns but I will call them Germans.

Jan. 15, 1915

My what a peaceful town Rockland and such a lovely parsonage, smaller than Caribou's. A nice kitchen and large dining area and a very spacious parlor. I am going to be at home here on 41 Beech Street. I am glad to have two bed rooms as I am sometimes in so much pain that I have to leave James' bed. He needs his sleep. I can catch up by sleeping late.

Jan. 18, 1915

We stayed at the Hotel Rockland until our furniture came. James will find someone to help get all the furniture in place before tomorrow, get the coal furnace going and the house warm before I sleep there.

Jan. 20, 1915

The Church had stocked the pantry with food for which I am thankful. It was very cold and James has not got a horse and wagon yet.

Jan. 30, 1915

James came home with a Morgan horse and a nice wagon with room in the back for lots of things. He named the gelding Bob. He has a bobbed tail. He looks quite intelligent. There is an attached barn for Bob and the wagon. I miss my Candy cat but right now we can get along without one. No hens either. James has preached his first sermon here. I did not go that first Sunday. I have been just a shade under the weather. Maybe soon I will feel better.

April 1, 1915

War! War! It is spring again and the newspapers are saying that the Triple Entente armies will be in Berlin before fall. More Canadians going overseas to fight. Letter today said the 68th annual Conference will be held in Dover April 14-19. I am going. It is my duty to go and help James as much as I can. It is rumored he will be the next D.S. And I turned 42 yesterday and James took me to the Thorndike Hotel for a grand evening. I had a salmon that was just perfect with a few clams first. James was picky; he had a lobster. Ice cream and cookies to finish with.

The sea is making me feel-------Oh well-------not really homesick but it sure takes me back a few years. James' birthday is soon – it is June first. I will invite all of the trustees and their wives and I will write a letter to Stella and ask for her help.

April 20, 1915

We had another overnight stay at the Bangor House going and coming from Dover. Bishop Joseph Berry is in favor on combining the Maine Conference and ours. He said that there was no need for two and it would save money for the Methodist Church. James has been convincing more and more people to this point of view. They are sending Isaac Lidstone to Caribou and Henry Marr to Mapleton and Washburn. The Charleses were there and we enjoyed them as we ate breakfast twice. I was made treasurer of the Women's Home Missionary Society. Charles Smith will be near for he is appointed to Camden. War news and mother's letter says that Burton and Isaiah Allen, George Smith, George and James Manship, Emma and Frank Barry, and Carl Berg have gone to be soldiers.

May 12, 1915

Stella has said she will come and spend a week with us and help in preparing James' birthday party. I am going to have clams and lobster -- no, they eat that all the time here. No -- I will have roast lamb like we had in Caribou when we went to the Sleeper store and they told me how to cook it -- I think I can find the recipe, it had rosemary as an herb -- and Mrs. Sleeper even told me how to fix the mint jell. I will have a leg of lamb, some new red potatoes and peas and carrots. A good onion soup to start would be right. Oh! I am glad Stella will be here to help.

May 20, 1915

We had the Mayor, Charles and Mrs. Harrington, Mr. and Mrs. I.L. Snow of the boat yard, and Mr. and Mrs. Caleb Moffit the surveyor. Mr. Snow had a right good laugh when I told him about my ocean going trip from Nova Scotia to Boston. Mrs. Ann Moffit offered that last summer she was so seasick on a trip to Boston on the Eastern Steamship steamers that she had to be put on the Maine Central to come home. She did not want to trespass on God's sea again. I said, "I am never-ever going on the sea, no, never." Mr. Moffit said, "The ride back on the train was much more pleasurable than the sea trip." Then we all sang Christian songs and some from theater shows. Mother's letter said many young men were going off to war. She said two Fillmore boys, William Boyce, Albert Carter, Roy Bradley, a Lamb boy -- maybe Harold, two Leger boys, Jim Godwin, Robert Hebert, Al and Will Walton.

Aug. 12, 1915

I have not picked a berry or looked for mushrooms. I am not in good enough health for that occupation. The War seems to go badly. The Germans are sinking ships without much concern for uninvolved passengers. I am hearing the blasting in the lime pits. I now know what it

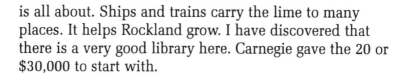

is all about. Ships and trains carry the lime to many places. It helps Rockland grow. I have discovered that there is a very good library here. Carnegie gave the 20 or $30,000 to start with.

Oct. 2, 1915

I have joined a literary group at the library. I am not able to march but I can do as many bake sales as I did in Caribou. I will just limit my efforts to the Ladies Aid of the Pratt Memorial Methodist Church. Yes and I just thought of it -- this is the second Methodist Church we have served that is dedicated to someone in the past, the Church in Hartland named in honor of Grace Linn and this Church named in honor of their pastor who spent his own money to make sure the roof had slate tiles to keep the rain out. Rev. George Pratt was a most loyal and devout pastor for the people of Rockland. Then they do talk about that Mrs. Harriet Eaton over in Livermore Falls who also gave money and her time to make sure they had a big beautiful Methodist church.

Dec. 4, 1915

Praise God -- the congress of the United States has outlawed the sale and dangerous use of opium without the doctor's order. President Wilson was for it. From what I read that is a great step forward in cutting back on robbery as a crime.

A letter from Mother tells about little Ray Raworth and his young friend John Munroe nearly drowning in the pond. They just had to skate on it and so they fell in. They are alive 'cause Old Uncle Silliker was driving by and had a long piece of rope in his pung. They were in luck, Uncle tossed the rope into the older boy's hands and told him to hang on with one hand and to grab the other boy by his jacket. Well they will live to skate again. Next time on firmer ice.

Jan. 2, 1916

The war continues. All of the British Empire have joined England in the war against Germany. Russia has been pushing at the backs of the GERMANS. I hope my friends in Canada are surviving the war. I am going to write mother and ask her for news of them. Many are overseas and some may have been killed or wounded.

Feb. 25, 1916

On the 23rd we had a monstrous snowstorm. It didn't stop for nearly two days. I am glad the pantry was well stocked and the barn had lots of hay and grain for Bob. He has been a very gentle horse. I am glad to have no outside jobs when it snows like it did. The Tibbets' market is going to send me my groceries. I can call them on the telephone.

March 10, 1916

Mother said in her letter that Courtney's woodworking place was doing war work and every man in the village was helping. More men have also gone to serve, Thorne Hayward, Warren Dobson, Amos Riley, James and Monsel Goodwin, Floyd Oulton, Carl Berg, Basil Johnston, and Fred Fitzpatrick.

April 5-9, 1916

James bought his first suit of clothes at Mayo and Rose. He is an accomplished tailor but did not find time to cut and sew a new suit for the conference. A practice he has been doing for some years. It looks very nice on my well built husband. It is more stylish than the ones he made.

We mostly took the cars to Camden every morning and came back every night. This was a most soul fulling conference. The Bishop John Hamilton is a great orator. You hear and understand every word. His message was most gratifying to James and his group that wants one conference for the state of Maine. James and the Bishop both work very diligently on this plan. The Bishop did not bring it to a vote but he sure made many converts for a one conference for Maine.

I spent some time with Rev. Robert Joscelyn who has been appointed to Caribou. I told him he would find them to be the friendliest Methodists in the state of Maine. Charles Jones is going to Hartland and Charles Smith to Union. Our new D.S. will be Carl Garland. He is going to the General Conference. My James hopes to go soon. We ate with David Tribou and the Charleses for breakfast twice.

Camden is a very pretty place and has many gorgeous homes. We hired a driver and wagon and did the tour.

July 6, 1916

We had a great parade on the 4th and I left the house to see it. James put me in the wagon and drove to a place on the march where I could see them going by. I have been in and out of bed since we went to the conference. We drove by the State Prison in Thomaston on our way back. 41 Beech is a fine house.

July 22, 1916

Yesterday and last night it rained and it rained and the wind came with such fury that old cedar shingles are all over the streets. Some children are gathering them for kindling.

Sept. 2, 1916

Stella came a month ago and has stayed here to help me get well. Now she has to go home and I will do the best I can in this house. I am not able to do the many things at the church. But I am going to go to the Sunday service. I have missed them for too long. I am going to ask James if he will help me into the wagon so I will not miss his services anymore.

Dec. 27, 1916

I have made it to most every service at Pratt Memorial and I am no sicker than I was before. So I am hoping God will see me through another year with my James. He has had a woman come twice a week to help with house work. James bought a stereoscopic viewer and some cards showing the Holy Land. They are most entertaining. How I wish my health would allow us to go there.

Jan. 24, 1917

I sent a note of thanks to Courtney for the nice cash present he sent us around Christmas. He also had to complain about the new taxes the government had to put on for the war. Court said he had lost several good young workers to the war effort. Frank McKay, Ivy Scott, Will Reilly, George Parks, Joseph Prescott, Walter Knapp, and Alonzo Goodwin.

April 7, 1917

U.S. of America Enters the War were the headlines in the paper James came home with. We are at war with Germany as of yesterday. Now we will be helping to defeat that bully who had intended to rule the world. The German Navy has been sinking passenger ships and they are brutalizing the people of Europe. My pain will have to be forgotten, for now we will all have to do our part in helping the Red Cross in their relief work. Lord, I am ready.

The Governor of State of Maine was right when he asked men to join the State Guard and start training some months ago.

April 20, 1917

I went with James to Bar Harbor on April 11-16. Bishop Frederick Leete sent Robert Joscelyn to Caribou, Charles Smith to Union and Charles Jones to Hartland, and James back to Rockland. I did not go to all the meetings but at the love feast I joined James in our testimony. James hired a horse-drawn cab and we did tour around some of the Bar Harbor fine homes.

June 12, 1917

Long letter from Mother. The boys are doing fine and the grandchildren are keeping her from being lonely. Yet she said I set the table with two plates half the time thinking Father is coming in from the shop. Word had come to the Port that Alvie Baker and John Berry are dead.

July 23, 1917

Mother sent me a list of some of the Port's war dead. I am going to write the families a letter. Will Boyce, Roy Bradley, Ivy Scott, Joseph Prescott, and Walt Knapp. The Munroe boys joined the army, and Carl and Sedley and Hugh Moore.

Sept. 2, 1917

The summer war has not yet come to a conclusion. I hope that God will see the misery of the men that live in cold muddy trenches and help bring this war to an end. The ships going to Europe are loaded with men and war supplies. Many arrive but some are sunk and many lives are lost. Sunk -- Yes -- we got a letter with the news that an old two-masted ship, the Willis & Guy, built in 1873, sank on the ledges of Pemaquid Point in a very dense fog. I will pray for safety at sea for our men -- no, for all men. Mother sent me a list of men's names who have been killed and wounded from the Port. I'll write to these families, Robert Hebert, Alonzo Goodwin, Will Riley, Fred Ibbistson, and Ray Duguay.

Dec. 12, 1917

The news that came today in our newspaper -- In my homeland at Halifax an ammunition ship exploded. I wanted to be angry at God for many innocent people were killed. Two ships collided in the harbor, one a Belgian carrying relief supplies, the other a French ship carrying ammunition. May God have mercy on those injured that survived though hurt. Lord be with the families of the 1500 killed by that mistake. We all pray for the end of this ruthless war.

Jan. 2, 1918

We have mice in the pantry and I am thinking on getting a cat. James must have guessed it and so he borrowed one from the market. He is a big gray one, a male I think, and he already thinks he owns the house. James said a borrowed cat would be best for the Bishop had whispered in his ear that he should not be surprised to be a D.S. this coming year.

Jan. 20, 1918

A letter from Mother and one from Reta. They both said the war has taken many from the Port and they may never come back as some they had heard had married girls from other places. Mother had these men sending letters home, Carl Berg, Fred Fitzpatrick, Basil Johnston, Clarence Mitton, Hugh Moore, Carl and Sedley Munroe. Thorne Hayward was reported dead but it was corrected.

Feb. 23, 1918

The letter came today -- the conference will be at Dexter April 9-14. I hope my health will allow me to go. I have not missed one. God willing I never will.

March 23, 1918

I sent the cat back, he had done his duty and we have no more mice in the pantry. The barn also may be mice-free as he spent his nights there. I have had the Literary group at my home now several times. It is a very interesting group of very intelligent ladies. I do not go to their home as my health is still very poorly.

April 3, 1918

Ernest sent a letter and Mother had hers in the same envelope. All are well and they are sure the war will soon be over. Several more have volunteered. I agree with many Canadians that to be fair they should have a draft somewhat like the States has.

April 15, 1918

I almost hate to pick up the newspaper or read my mail. The war goes on and the end is still not in sight. I and all the world prays that soon the guns will be silent and that all those young men will return to their loved ones and homes. I have and will write letters to all the families that have lost a son in the several towns that we have served. I have the local papers sent to me. All theaters are closed in the state because so many people have died of influenza.

April 20, 1918

I had a very hard time at the conference in Dexter. Charles Jones and Charles Smith visited me at the hotel. I made very few of the meetings. And now I am in bed. I have asked James to call Stella and ask her to come help me for a few days. Stella takes over your house but she is such a comfort. She is a good friend and takes good care of my dear James.

April 22, 1918

Stella came and the house is being taken care of and she has made me comfortable. And she has spent time with me in reminiscing. Stella joins us in the morning with our worship -- right after breakfast.

May 20, 1918

I feel much better. The sun is warm and the flowers are blooming. Stella stayed here for two weeks and I gained more strength every day. We are packing for

Bangor. James is the District Super. He has sold Bob and the wagon. My spirits are soaring.

May 22, 1918

We are in our home here in Bangor, 125 Grove Street. I am going to bed, the trip was very tiring. James will have to hire someone to do the house work or do it himself.

May 25, 1918

I did go to the Dexter Conference. I have never missed one. I must admit that this was a most difficult one for me and James. I had to be helped most of the time. A train ride to Dexter was most difficult. Yet I would not have stayed away for I was very determined to hear each service and be a part of the continuing work to extend God's Kingdom but I could not go to them all. I will ask Mrs. McNaught, thanks to James she is here, for some hot milk and that may let me sleep after I say my prayers. James comes into my room later when I am nearly asleep and kisses me. I always feel him coming when he enters my bed room.

May 30, 1918

I have been recieving the Aroostook Republican now for a few years. I spend most of the day in bed now. I have Mrs. McNaught bring me paper and ink. I have written to all those families who have lost sons in the war. It is my intention to write to each member family of the church in Caribou, also to all my friends in the G.A.R. and the Women's Relief Corps. I know that I will soon be meeting my maker. James can mail these letters then. "I'd like some tea Mrs. McNaught."

June 1, 1918

I am still in my bed. The Doctor has changed my medicine again. My pain has not ceased and poor James has had to carry on without a bit of help from me. I got another letter from Mother. I am so glad she is well and healthy. I wanted to write to the parents of the young people who drowned but have not the strength. As soon as I can I will. That latest pill has caused me to doze and so I'll stop now.

June 12, 1918

I got a letter today from Mrs. Mita Poland. Among her news was a very welcome line that Austin Poland, a great grand son of Ansel G. Taylor, on June sixth raised the flag on our 82-foot pole over the Monument and then the Monument was unveiled. So my few words spoken about a monument that had appealed to me in Boston turned out to start this good project. How I would have liked to have been there.

Too many letters come from our friends from the past assignments telling us of loss or injury of their sons in this war.

June 16, 1918

I fell on my knees and prayed and prayed -- after I read the news in the Caribou Republican of that fatal accident. I cried until no more tears would come. May our God comfort their families. And Jesus, I need your comfort because four of my lovely young men and women drowned on the 9th of June. I had led them in Sunday School. James will be devastated for he had brought all of them to know the Lord. Mona Davis, a very charming beautiful girl, not quite 16. Georgia Lyons just 17 of the James Lyons family. Max Simpson just 17 and the son of Mrs. Frank Simpson and David Hitchings 18 and the son of Mr. and Mrs. Herbert Hitchings. They had over a thousand people at the funeral in the Peoples M.E. church. Service was conducted by all the local ministers, Joscelyn, Bishop, Minor, and Cheney. Those children were in a canoe and were sailing and it was reported the girls stood up to exchange seats and they all fell into 15

feet of cold water. Not all the news from Caribou
Methodists and the other Churches we have served are
tragic -- the new births, the weddings and the happy
times news help me to open the newspaper as it arrives. I
will write a letter of sympathy to the families if my pain
will ease up some. I am going to have the evening meal
with James tonight. It has been a while since I have felt
up to that much time in a chair at our table.

June 30, 1918

My, Oh My! The Republican has the sad news of war.
Donald Sutherland was killed. He was a young Marine
and a good Methodist. I shall write his parents a letter
today.

July 20, 1918

I got a letter from a friend of our former church.
Henry Pratt, such a nice boy, was killed on July 18. He
was not born in Caribou but we all liked this one very
much. Even though I never met his parents I plan on
writing them. Henry helped me in Caribou to do some
odd jobs. Such a happy boy.

August 20, 1918

From the Republican, Joseph Nadeau. I'll have to write
and ask for his parents' name and address. He died of the
flu.

October 2, 1918

The Republican reported that Perley Palmer was killed
in action. I know his parents and I will write.

October 10, 1918

I have had a bad relapse and now will be in bed for
some time. I am only going to write my friends letters
when I am up to it. James will mail them when I am with
my Jesus in Heaven. I know I am sick and I pain so much

that I hope my passing will not be delayed too much more. Now I will speak to God.

FINAL

October 18, 1919

James came with some food about noon and I did my best to eat some. We prayed together and he told me again that he had loved me and hoped to keep on for yet a long long time. I fell asleep and woke to the rain beating on the window and my body is in pain. Pain that has grown until I want to scream like the banshees of Hell but I will not let it leave my throat. That would only cause dear dear James to call the old Doctor again and it will cause my James pain. Dr. Webster was just here this morning and I took his medicine to help and it did for a few hours.

I do feel that the Lord will call me soon and I am ready to shut out this pain.. We have done the Lord's work. James and I have been in his hands all our lives. I am willing to rest in the Lord's hands. Let the pain leave me, Lord, let the pain leave. More medicine and this hymn is racing through my head. My head! Thank you Lord and Saviour

Obituary

MRS. JAMES H. GRAY

Funeral services for Mrs. James Gray were held from the First Methodist church in Bangor at 2 o'clock Tuesday, October 21, 1919. The service was most impressive and was conducted by the Rev. A.E. Morris of the First Methodist. Mrs. Gray died at her home after a long illness. Mrs. Gray was, before her marriage, Miss Bessie Beatrice Raworth, daughter of the late Silliker Raworth and Mrs. Millicent Dobson Raworth. She was born in Port Elgin, New Brunswick, Canada March 31, 1873. She married July 6, 1892 to Rev. James H. Gray of Port Elgin. Mr. and Mrs. Gray came to Maine 20 years ago, residing first in Cushing. Rev. Gray's ministering has taken them to Rockport, Boothbay Harbor, Hartland, Caribou and Rockland. The Grays have resided in this city as he was the superintendent of the Eastern District of the East Maine Conference.

Mrs. Gray is survived by her husband, her mother, Mrs. Millicent Raworth of Port Elgin, brothers Courtney and Ernest of New Brunswick. A sister Mrs. Avery (Reta) Oulton of Baie Verte, N.B.

A former Superintendent of the Bangor District of the Eastern District wrote these lines about Bessie. "I frequently enjoyed the hospitality of Mrs. Gray, and it was with pleasure that I welcomed her to First Methodist of Bangor. Her willingness to help to the limit of her physical ability, her pleasing personality, and her cheerful word won her a large place in the affections of her people. Her death was a keen sorrow to these many friends."

The service was most impressive and was conducted by the Rev. A.E. Morris, pastor of the First M.E. Church. The organ music was played by Mrs. Grace Bramhall Howes. Scripture was read by Rev. C.W. Lowell of Howland, and Rev. A.J. Lockhart of Winterport. Rev. March of Old Town sang two beautiful anthems. For the Conference, Rev. A.E. Luett, Superintendent of the Western District of the Maine Conference preached. Rev. C.J. Brown delivered the eulogy. The entire service was one which, though simple, was made impressive. The service started with the congregation singing "For All the Saints" and ended with the same hymn. For they all knew that Bessie was "A SAINT." There were many beautiful flowers, mostly blue, some from every church they had pastored. The bearers were The Reverends George Gorwood, Brewer; W.O. Genge, Grace Methodist; D.M. Angell, Bucksport; T.S. Ross, Lincoln; L.D. Porter, Eddington; H.D. Sellers, Orono; George Richardson, Vanceboro; Lew Pressey, Danforth; Richard Moyle, Ellsworth; C.F. Prudy, Winterport; C.F. Beebee, Orrington; Rev. Mayo, Addison; Rev. Swapp, Columbia.

Close friends of the Grays, Rev. Charles Jones and Rev. Charles Smith, sat with Rev. Gray at the service. Rev. Gray accompanied the body back to the family in Port Elgin, N.B. Burial will take place in the Raworth family plot.

A True Copy of the Message Sent to the Secretary of State

Voted at the Fourth Quarterly Conference of the People's Methodist Episcople Church of Caribou, Maine, held at the Church building at said Caribou on e Twelfth day of December A.D. 1919, that said conference approved the changing of its said Church name from The People's Methodist Episcople Church to the Bessie Gray Memorial Church.

> Sgd. Carlotta P. Keyes
> Secretary of the fourth Quarterly
> Conference of Caribou People's
> Methodist Episcople Church

Fee paid to Secretary of State $5.00

Jan. 1, 1920
125 Grove
Bangor, Maine

My Dear Mrs. H.D. Ebbett,

I have been meaning to write and have you thank all those great Methodists in Caribou that have honored my wife Bessie by naming your beautiful church in her memory. I am deeply moved by this action.

Now I want to tell you about that last day Bessie and I had together. She has been very ill for the last four years and so she had an upstairs bedroom all to herself. Now I have called many doctors to Bessie's side and I had called Doctor Webster several times since coming to Bangor. Although I was not anxious. I called the operator on that great invention of Mr. Bell's. I had only to say who I was and the doctor said, "I will be right over."

I then took myself to the kitchen to make my oatmeal breakfast. While I was eating this I reminisced about the many times Bessie and I had this food. It was rare when we changed our breakfast. Then I remembered all the late night snacks of the leftover morning oatmeal. It was quickly prepared after all those late night meetings that Methodist ministers have nearly every day of the year.

Just as I cleaned the breakfast dishes since Mrs. McNaught had the day off to go see a sick sister, the doorbell rang. As I opened the door to a cheery voiced Doctor, I thought about the first words this healer of bodies had greated this healer of souls with. "Yes, I am still using a horse and buggy because if the good Lord wanted us to go as fast as those confounded automobiles, why he would have provided us with a horse that could run that fast. I am very pleased, thank you. I like to travel at a good pace behind my trusted mare, Julia. She always takes me and brings me home." Then the Doctor handed me his coat and said to hang it where it could dry as his buggy had a leak in the roof. He turned and abruptly climbed the stairs to Bessie's room. I then did some household chores and read some in the morning paper. When Doctor Webster came back down, I offered him a cup of coffee and was surprised when he accepted. He had always made the excuse that he had had one cup which was his daily allowance.

When I poured he stirred the sugar and cream thoroughly before he started to speak.

"James – James – your wife Bessie – is not – she is – James, she is desperately ill James – and we physicians are not going to be able to keep her alive much longer. She is in the Lord's hands. I have done all that we physicians can do."

He left most of the coffee in the cup and after seeing him to the door and helping him into his dry coat, I went to my room and prayed. I took Bessie some breakfast which I helped her eat, and then she fell into a sleep. I then went to my study and checked the calender, Monday, the 20th of October, 1919.

I found that I was to meet with two young seminarians who want some experience at preaching. We have several small churches in the outskirts of Bangor who depend on these students to do their preaching. I did that at 10:30 at the seminary.

I had another meeting at noon with the president of the seminary. I was recommending a student from Rockland. Next I wrote letters to several pastors on matters of church discipline.

I came back to the house around 2 p.m. and found Bessie still asleep. Then I worked at the forms that must be filled out for the Bishop. I really like this part of the work and am glad that Bessie never wanted to do this for me. She was much more effective in leadership of church members and she surely made the Methodists well-known in every pastorate I had. Most of my ministerial friends envied me of my Bessie's women's work. At three-thirty I climbed the stairs and then came right back down and called the good Doctor Webster who came and said my Bessie had gone to be with her Lord and was in no more need of this doctor's medicine. When the undertaker came he asked me, "What dress should Bessie have on in the casket?"

Now I remember her as a bride, and searched my mind for where Bessie might have put this dress. I started looking through her dresser and soon discovered her diary and a pile of letters she had asked me to mail on her death. There were condolences to the families – in the villages and towns we had pastored in – who had lost sons in the war. I then went to the closet and the top shelves had several old boxes that a dress might have been laid out in. On the first try I found the blue wedding dress! I cried over it but took it down for my Bessie to put on her body. Her soul is now in heaven, and how I will miss my blue-gowned bride and life-mate. I took her body back to Port Elgin and visited with her family. Her mother, brother and sisters were there to grieve with me.

I again want to write my thanks to all the church members, and very soon I will send you our separate

portraits which were taken here in Bangor a few years
ago.

May His love be with you always and may you grow
in the spiritual things every day.

In Christian Love and Friendship,
James H. Gray

You may pass this letter to all.

A brief resume of James' life after Bessie and some of
his obituary.

At the Dexter, Maine Conference of April 1918, James
was appointed Superintendent of the Eastern District of
the Methodist Eastern Maine Conference. He moved with
Bessie from Rockland to the D.S. House on 125 Grove
Street, Bangor, where Bessie died.

James traveled with her body to Port Elgin, New
Brunswick. There she was buried in the Raworth family
plot.

In April 1919 at the Milo, Maine Conference, James
was reappointed D.S. for the Bangor District. At the
Brewer 1920 Conference, James reported his address as
P.O. Box 737 to Bishop Hughes. After he was given the
D.S. job for the Bangor District, he lived on 10 Hudson,
Bangor. This year James went to the General Conference
in Des Moines, Iowa. The General Conference opened on
May 3, 1920. On this travel he missed his Bessie most
every minute of that trip as he was going to a strange
land.

Bishop Hughes at the April 1921 Conference sent
James to Boothbay Harbor to be the Western District D.S.
While there James married Stella D. Hodgdon on April 27,
1921.

In April 1922, at the East Maine Conference, James
and many of his followers celebrated the finalized union
with the Maine Conference. He had seen the fulfillment
of his dream – *one conference for all of Maine.*

May 4th on Sunday morning in 1925 as the Boothbay Harbor church bells called the earthly children of God to worship, James heard the Heavenly call and peacefully and quietly slipped away to be an attendant at the Father's House on High.

L.D. Porter wrote his obituary:

Rev. James Hanford Gray, second son of John and Rachel Gray of New-Castle-on-Tyne, England, was born June first, 1868.

At the age of thirteen, he moved with the family; immigrating to Prince Edward Island. At the age of twenty-seven, he came to Boston to enter school. He recieved his early education in England, his secondary and college work at Mount Allison University, New Brunswick and his theological training at Boston School of Theology.

He was married July 6th, 1892, to Bessie Raworth of Port Elgin, New Brunswick. She was his constant co-worker until she answered the call to come up higher, October 20, 1919. He was married to Stella D. Hodgdon of Boothbay Harbor, Maine, on April 17, 1921. She lives to mourn him. Stella ministered unto him in his failing health supplying every possible comfort and ease.

He was an able and powerful preacher, a wise counsellor, and a devoted pastor. He had an optimisim that was an inspiration and a social genius and culture that made him popular, lovable and winsome. He was an undefatigable worker, never sparing himself, but using his versatile qualities for the Kingdom of God.

He fought for years the disease that finally brought on his death. He worked, however, until his strength completely failed. With the tenacity that was charac-teristic of him, he would work and correspond on his couch until he could no longer endure it.

The funeral services were conducted in the home in Boothbay Harbor by Rev. L.G. March, D.S. of the District, assisted by E.V. Allen, F.E. Smith, C.N. Garland, and L.D. Porter. The internment was in Ocean View, Boothbay.

Women Honored by the
United Methodist Church

ALABAMA

Julia Street Memorial UMC., P.O. Box 496 Boaz, AL. 35957 The sun was brilliant that day in 1891, inspiring Reverend J.T. Black to begin the delightful task of organizing a Methodist Episcopal church in South Boaz. In 1917 interest was high to build a NEW, LARGER church, and the architects were leaving out the church bell. A small widow with a dissenting voice arose in the meeting and said, "A church bell is the voice of the church to my community, and I think the bell should stay..." The present brick structure has the bell in an obscure northeast turret. No longer does it ring, but in 1943 this east side Methodist Church's parishioners renamed their church in honor of the "Lady of the Bell" who had been a devout member until her death in 1935.

Walker Memorial UMC of Elyton, AL. was organized in 1816 in the home of James Owen and was first known as Elyton Methodist Episcopal Church. Elyton was a village in present day Birmingham which was incorporated in 1871. The log cabin church on Broad Street had Dr. T.G. Slaghter as the first pastor. The name was changed in 1910 when the congregation moved to a new building on High or Main Street. At that time they named the church after Corilla Margaret Porter (Mrs. William A. Walker) because of her work in that Christian vineyard. Born March 21, 1824, in Monevallo, Shelby, Al.; died Nov. 1, 1908 in Elyton, Jefferson, Al. She was the granddaughter of Mitchell Porter and Penelope West, early Methodists on the American frontier. A larger church was built in 1924 but closed in 1989.

Whitefield UMC 2673 Fisk Rd., Montgomery, AL 36111 Al. Church named after Willie V. Whitfield of the Whitfield Pickle Company.

ALASKA – none

ARIZONA – none

ARKANSAS

Theressa Hoover UMC on 4000 West 13th Street in Little Rock, AR., 72204. This unusual church came from an empty U.M.C. building whose congregation moved. A far-sighted man by the name of Rev. William Robinson Jr. opened the old door in 1980. He selected this name when the church was charted in 1981. Theressa Hoover was a native of Fayetteville and had been long active in UMC missions programs. Rev. Robinson wanted the new congregation to "Minister to the whole community," and not just be the congregation. The Theressa Hoover church formed a nonprofit organization, *Black Community Developers, Inc. (BCD)*. Day care to homeless shelter has made this U.M.C. a leader in Christian activities in Little Rock.

Hazel Edwards Memorial UMC Newark, AR. The church was organized in 1886. Mr. Tomlinson gave the land. That church burned and a new one was built in 1923. The new church was named to honor the daughter of C.M. Edwards, who left a sizable legacy at the time of his death in 1957.

Hinton UMC, RR 3 Box 51A, Prescott, AR., 71857. Organized in 1913 in the Hinton schoolhouse. It was built on land donated by Mrs. Jake Hinton. A new church was built in 1957 using the old church material, and it is two miles east of the early church.

Mary Greenhaw Memorial UMC, P.O. Box 389, Marshall, AR., 72645. Organized in 1880 they met in the Plank Schoolhouse which sat east of the cemetery on College Street. The church was built in 1885 on land donated by Mary Greenhaw.

CALIFORNIA – none

COLORADO
Hess Memorial Church at East 31st Ave. and Elizabeth Street, Denver, CO. Nina Cobb Hess gave the first $500 for the church building. It is closed now.

Amanda K. Alger Memorial 303 Maple, Eaton, CO. 80614. Now called the First Methodist Church of Eaton. Amanda left a memorial fund which helped to build the first church building.
Lousia Hopkins Memorial ME Church. 203 E. 5th Street, Ovid, CO., 80744. Now known as the Ovid UMC.

CONNECTICUT
Mary Taylor UMC 168 Broad St., Milford, CT., 06460. Mary Anne Meyer born 1842 in N.J., oldest of seven of John Christopher Meyer of Hanover, Germany and Margaretta Evans of Welch descent. Mary married Henry Augustus Taylor of New York City. Four of their eight children died young. Mary died in 1878. Her remains were brought from Charlottesville, NY to Woodlawn Cemetery in Milford. Mary never lived in Milford but the Taylor's had an estate there (Lauralton Hall).
Mr. Taylor overheard some servants complaining about the rundown condition of their Methodist church. He was an Episcopalian but his wife was said to be a Methodist. On April 15, 1891 the Methodist pastor, James A. Macmillan, came to Lauralton Hall and was offered money to build a new edifice that was to be donated by Mary's children. Ground breaking was on March 15, 1892 and the Cornerstone laid October 3, 1892, dedicated June 25, 1893. The Mary Taylor Memorial Methodist Episcopal Church is a magnificent stone structure.

FLORIDA
Epperson Memorial UMC 7541 Lem Turner Road, Jacksonville, FL., 3207-0336. We find among the 34

Charter members was Sidney I. Sneller, who deeded land on the Turner Road for the church on Nov. 18, 1930. On September 10, 1931, the congregation changed the name from Oakhurst to Epperson Memorial Methodist Church in memory of Sidney's mother, Mrs. Nancy Epperson Sneller – a devout woman. We have one of her written prayers (1881), "...It is my desire to be fully consecrated to God, soul and body, time, talent, influence, love and all I would consecrated to the will and the work of the Lord..."

Swaim Memorial UMC 1620 Naldo Ave., Jacksonville, FL., 3207-336. Mrs. Elizabeth Caroline Booth Swaim had the title of "Church Mother." She was a charter member of the then Grace Methodist Episcopal. Grace had its beginning in 1886 in the home of Mrs. Swaim. She was born in 1866 in Barrie, Ontario, Canada and died in 1924.

Wagg Memorial UMC 4401 Garden Ave., West Palm Beach, FL., 33405-2541. Sarah Wagg was the wife of the Rev. Alfred H. Wagg. The church had its start in the 1921 Florida real estate boom. Leading citizens, Dr. C.K. Vieit, Dr. Alfred H. Wagg, Senator Alfred H. Wagg 2nd and Howard Selby organized a Methodist Church in South Palm Beach. Dr. Wagg's son, Alfred, who was a local real estate developer gave the money for the first temporary building, which was called the Sarah Wagg Methodist Church. This building was used while the permanent Spanish-styled building was constructed on Kaye and Garden Avenues. This is where the Sarah Wagg Memorial United Methodist Church of today is located.

Carlson Memorial UMC in LaBell, Hendry County, FL. The following is written by Geraldine Rue of that congregation.
"Swen Robert Emmanuel Carlson moved to LaBell in 1930 to serve LaBell Methodist Church. He was from Rockford, IL., where he was raised in the Swedish

Lutheran Church. He moved to Groveland, FL., joined the Methodist Church in 1924, and was ordained a deacon in 1933, elder in 1934.

Maud Corinna Magill was a beloved local teacher who had lived in LaBell most, if not all of her life. They met, married December 20, 1931. Bob served the church until June of 1935 when he was transferred to the church at Islamorado on Matecumbe Key.

On September 2, 1935 the most powerful hurricane ever to hit the United States struck the Florida Keys (the famous Labor Day Hurricane), and Bob and Maud were killed as they tried to help church members board up their homes and get to safety. Their gravesite is in Groveland.

In the meantime, the church at LaBell was suffering the aftermath of the great depression, and was close to losing the church to mortgage default. The church was actually padlocked at one time, and the congregation met in a nearby school.

The families of Bob and Maud Carlson, who had no children, gave their insurance money to the church, and that money combined with donations from statewide congregations, paid off the mortgage, and on April 11, 1937 the church was dedicated debt-free to the memory of the Carlsons."

GEORGIA

Ruth's Chapel UMC, Tarrytown, GA., 30470. Named after the wife of Charles S. Hamilton. It was organized in 1889. Services took place in Ruth's Chapel Schoolhouse. Charles S. Hamilton deeded the land for the church on Dec. 2, 1890. The church was completed early in 1891 and rebuilt after a storm at a new location on land that was given by Mrs. Millie Smith on the Thompson Pond Road in Montgomery County.

Lewis Memorial UMC 5555 Hereford Farm Road, Evans, GA., 30809. This church was founded by Mrs.

William Ellis Lewis in 1900. Her husband gave the land. In 1947 the Quarterly Conference changed the name from Sardis to Lewis in honor of Mrs. Lewis.

Lucy Chapel 1785 Old Prospect Church Road, Jeffersonville, GA., 31044. Named after the daughter of Colonel Daniel G. Hughes who helped build the church.

Martha Bowman Memorial UMC in Macon, GA., 31210. This church has gone from one location to another and has had three names. Before the Civil War the Damascus church was out in the country. When it moved in town after the war, Sarah Bowman Johnson asked that the Damascus name stay with the old country church for their yearly reunions. The new church was named Wilma after a banker who made substantial contributions.

In 1938 Dr. S.L. Akers, who was the Dean of Wesleyan College in Macon, persuaded the congregation to honor the Bowman Family, and Martha was chosen to represent them. On May 5, 2001 the church celebrated its 100th year by praising the past and present members and asking the Holy Spirit's guidance for the future.
E-mail: themoons@eagnet.com.

Pearson's Chapel, Star Route, Reidsville, GA. Named after Elizabeth Richardson Pearson. Organized in 1868. The original building is still in use and in good condition.

Ruth's Chapel, Vidalia and Zadee Roads, Montgomery County, GA. Charlie Hamilton gave the land and the church was built in 1891. Ruth was Mr. Hamilton's wife.

Rosebud, 4842 Weley Woods Drive, Macon, GA., 31210 named after Rose, the daughter of B.S. Fitzpatrick: discontinued in 1987 D.S. Cynthia Hooks Autry e-mail: macons@juna.com.

Crosby Chapel, 1759 Red Oak Road, Baxley, GA., 31513. Named after Mrs. Ada Crosby who gave the land for the church. Pastor Craig Smith's e-mail: chooper@cybersouth.com.

Harper Chapel, 277 Ben Carter Road, Baxley, GA., 31512. Named after Mrs. Haggai Harper who gave the land for the church. Pastor: Wayne Rogers.

Lelia Chapel, 600 East 12th Street, Tifton, GA., 31794. is named after the wife of an early pastor. Charles Rooks is the pastor.

Elizabeth Chapel, P.O. Box 177, Alma, GA., 31510 is named after Elizabeth Taylor, wife of the founder. Pastor: Ronnie Howell.

Martha Memorial UMC, 2616 Winchester Road, Waycross, GA., 31503. Named after the founder's mother, Mrs. Martha Smith. Pastor: Lonzie Wester.

Mary Branan UMC, 1776 Sylvan Road, Atlanta, GA., 30310. Mary Allen Lindsey Branan was a charter member of the Evans Chapel and the Woman's Missionary Society and a very active member of her church until her death. Her son C.I. Branan in his will established the Mary Allen Lindsey Branan Foundation "as a tribute to his mother who was left a widow with seven small children to raise." Born Dec. 24, 1830, lived until Dec. 9, 1915. Two daughters and two sons survived her. This church was the result of the merger of Mary Branan UMC and the UMC of Sylvan Hills in 1944.

HAWAII – none

IDAHO – none

ILLINOIS
Alice Chapel in Philo circuit in Champaign County, Illinois was named after Alice Babb Helm. It stood across

the road from Lynn Grove Cemetery. Church was razed in 1905.

Ellen Moore UMC in Fairfield, 1205 Hawkins Drive, IL., 62837-1034 at the corner of Seventh and Delaware.

From their records, "There was a time when there were no churches in the west part of Fairfield. A group of Christian people started a Sunday school on Feb. 19, 1896 in the home of Joseph Sloan. They met that first day at 2:00 p.m., and the lesson was the birth of Moses. Sunday school soon outgrew this home and moved to an inter-denominational Sunday school on 606 W. Main Street.

By the spring of 1901 a new building was needed, but very little money was available. Ellen Moore, the little daughter of Daltie and Mollie Moore had died. Ellen was born August 14,1893, and died December 20, 1900. Her mother remembered how Ellen had watched the children pass their house going to Sunday school and had said, "Oh, Mother, I wish we could build them a church."

So Mr. and Mrs. Daltie Moore offered to give $500 toward building a church to be called the Ellen Moore Mission as a living memorial to their daughter. Ellen's grandfather Land Wall gave $500, Mrs. J.Q. Rapp gave $100…Sam McAtee sold the land for $50 and gave $25 back.

A new church in 1939 has Ellen's picture and the stone bearing her name. Her mother Mollie was able to attend this dedication service. After another sanctuary was built in 1962 the older building was used for Sunday school, assembly hall and preacher's study.

INDIANA
The Breaden Memorial UMC in Terre Haute, IN. Named after co-pastors Charles Calvin and Kate Breaden.

IOWA – none

KANSAS

Susanna Wesley UMC 7433 SW 29th St. Wichita, KS., 66614-4700. All UMC people know that she was the mother of John and Charles. This church began in 1984 as a Mission, chartered on January 20, 1985. It is located next to Aldersgate Village – a UMC retirement community. With land from Aldersgate Village and $75,000 from Kansas East Conference they constructed their first church in 1990. The church continued to grow and by 1996 they had erected another church building. Now in 2001, they are planning a new church building at 37th and Auburn Road. The land has been purchased. E-mail: swumc@cjnetworks.com. Visit them at www.swumc.org.

KENTUCKY

Betsy Layne, P.O. Box 155, Carisle, KY., 42404-0155. E-mail: mwallen@kymt.net.

Webb Mem. UMC, 370 St. Route 100 N, Clay, KY., 42404. The church was named after Eliza Webb. Her father was a prominent businessman, in western Kentucky (Owensboro?) and when the congregation at Clay decided to build, he gave a significant monetary gift and asked that the church be named in honor of his mother.

LOUISIANA

The Lea Joyner Memorial UMC, 4390 Old Sterlington Road, Monroe, LA., 71203. Fax: (318) 343-9528. Named after Rev. Lea Joyner, the pastor of Southside UMC for thirty years. Born June 17, 1919 in Natchez MI., but claimed Grayson, LA. as her home. Lea preached to her dolls and never wavered in her plan to become a pastor for God and the Methodists. She was ordained on Jan. 1st 1939 and was pastor to many. Dr. Joiner was one of the early ordained Methodist ministers to serve the church she had organized. In 1980 she was in Southside UMC office and was abducted. Several days later they found her body.

Southside UMC was organized in 1952 with 126 members. In 1980 they had a membership of 2200 with a property valued at three million dollars. Lea had been their only pastor. To fully grasp this woman's love of ministering to people, you would need to read Harry Hale Jr's book, "Standing in the Gap, the life and ministry of, the Rev. Lea Joyner." Southside was dedicated for the memory of this very remarkable Christian woman.

The Elizabeth Sullivan Memorial UMC, P.O. Box 1143, Bogalusa, LA., 70429. Elizabeth was wife of Col. W.H. Sullivan – the founder of The Great Southern Lumber Co. in Bogalusa who donated land for the Methodist and Catholic churches. They joined the First Methodist in 1907. The name was changed Aug. 27, 1922 after Col. Sullivan presented them with a pipe organ in memory of his wife. The community hospital is also called the Elizabeth Sullivan.

MAINE

Gray Memorial UMC, 8 Prospect Street, Caribou, ME., 04736. The Bessie Gray Memorial UMC, my home church is the idea that the author started with in writing this book.

Brown Memorial UMC, 15 Church Street, P.O. Box 58, Clinton, ME., 04927. Jonathan Brown came to Clinton in 1802 and started classes, first in his home then in the schoolhouse. In 1884 it was necessary to expand to a church building. On Jan. 4, 1885 it was dedicated as the Brown Memorial Methodist Episcopal Church in memory of Jonathan and Betsy Brown. (Roots and Wings by Patricia J. Thompson, 1993.)

Grace Linn UMC on Upper Commercial Street. P.O. Box 418, Hartland, ME., 04928. In 1860 Archibald and

Grace, with their four children, came from Scotland to Hartland. They brought machinery and workers and established the Linn Woolen Mill. Grace, a devout Methodist, soon organized a Methodist congregation and in 1883 the church was constructed and dedicated on March 26, 1884. The first service was Grace Linn's funeral. The church was soon named the Grace Linn Memorial Methodist Episcopal Church.

Eaton Memorial UMC, P.O. Box 353, Livermore Falls, ME., 04254. From a church historical booklet we find Harriet Eaton has her birthday on January 14, in 1820, died on September 24, 1917. John Eaton was a trustee when the church was moved from Stone's Corner to Livermore Falls. Lumber for underpinning the old church for this move came from the Eaton farm. In April 1905 the congregation under Rev. George Howard accepted a pipe organ and decided to build a new church. The new church has a stained glass window to honor the John W. and Harriet N. Eaton family. On January 5, 1911, the church was dedicated by Rev. J.A. Bethcher and Rev. George Howard.

"Eaton Memorial Methodist Episcopal Church," is named in honor of Mrs. Harriet Eaton who had contributed most toward the building of the church.

MARYLAND
Baldwin Memorial UMC, 921 General Highway, Millersville, MD., 21108-2124. On Thanksgiving Day in 1896 a lovely granite church, the third building, was dedicated and the Baltimore Annual Conference, over the protests of the donors (the children of William and Jane Baldwin) changed the name from Cross Roads to Baldwin Memorial, honoring Mr. and Mrs. William Henry Baldwin.

Alberta Gary Memorial UMC, 5305D Columbia Rd., Columbia, MD., 21044. Edward and Emily Spedden gave the "old Patterson Farm" for a church. This donation was to be voided if the church was not erected in two years.

In 1871 when James Albert Gary (1833-1920) learned of the effort to build a church in Columbia, he made a very large contribution with one request: it was to be named after his daughter, who had died at the age of five (a photo shows her to be a pretty one). This owner of the Guilford Mills became Postmaster General under President McKinley.

Fanny Lowe Memorial Methodist Protestant Church in Talbot County, MD. Erected in 1895 and closed and demolished by 1941. From Geo. Caley of Smyrna, Delaware.

MICHIGAN – none

MINNESOTA

Janet Hill UMC, Pastor Roy Vanderwerf, P.O. Box 98, McGregor MN., 55760-0098. Phone: (218) 697-2662. E-mail: lkohlgraf@juno.com. The church was named Janet C. Hill Memorial as a window had been given by Mr. Hill, who was referred to as a railroad man.

MISSISSIPPI

Dantzler Memorial, Moss Point, MS. This church, also known as First United Methodist Church of Moss Point, was named the Sarah Eran Dantzler. The church was organized in 1852. The present building was erected in 1914, a gift from the Dantzler family in memory of their mother.

Emmanuel UMC, Jacksonville, MS. Originally named the Bessie Shands Mission, the church was formed in 1932 as an outreach mission of the Women's Bible Class of Grace Methodist, the downtown Jacksonville church.

Twelve-year-old Louise Axton was teaching Sunday school under an oak tree when Mrs. Eunice Langley drove down the street in 1932. She stopped and asked if she could come back next Sunday and join them. This Sunday school grew, and soon Mrs. Bessie Shands, wife of a doctor, donated a house to be used by the mission. Located in South Jacksonville, it grew from its Sunday school beginnings, and after Mrs. Shands death it was named the Bessie Shands Memorial Methodist in 1915, then renamed to Emmanual UMC in 1973 or 74.

Ethel UMC, Ethel, MS. Originally known as Stonewall, a railroad official renamed the community for his daughter. So the church has the daughter's name. The Methodist church was organized in 1884.

Faith, UMC, 4005 Chieot Road, Pascagoula, MS., 39581. This church was once named Becky Bacot, named after the daughter of the church benefactor. She was killed in a car accident while a college student. When it was founded in 1958 it was named Bayou Casotte Methodist. It changed to Lakeside Methodist in 1959 and then to Becky Bacot in 1960. In 1990 it took the present name.

Mamie C. Weaver Memorial UMC, 1416 Mather Diamond, Waynesboro, MS., 39397. Organized in 1920, was earlier known as Chapperall Methodist. Church is located on 5 Mamie Weaver Avenue.

Valena C. Jones UMC, Bay St. Louis, MS. Founded in 1810 as St. Paul Methodist Episcopal Church, the name was changed to Valena C. Jones in 1926 when a new building was erected and dedicated to the sacred memory of Mrs. Jones. This historically black church was named for the wife of MEC Bishop Robert E. Jones of Greensboro, NC, who presided over the New Orleans area in the Central Jurisdiction. Mrs. Jones was a native of Bay St. Louis and her parents were among the founders of the church.

MISSOURI

Culbertson Chapel UMC. In 1893 Mrs. A.J. Culbertson gave the land to build a church at Stewartsville, MO., 64490.

MONTANA – none

NEBRASKA

Pearl Memorial UMC, 2319 Ogden, Omaha, NE., 68110. On September 1906 a contract was made for a building to fulfill a growing need of the Methodists in the area north of Ames Ave.

In September 1906 the building was started and by July 28, 1907 it was known as the "North 24th Street Methodist Episcopal Church". Growing again forced the congregation to plan a new church. A lot was purchased on 24th and Ogden and the building was started by July 15, 1918 and was dedicated on Dec. 4, 1927. The congregation renamed the church to honor Rev. and Mrs. George Luce, Pearl being Mrs. Luce's maiden name.

St. Luke UMC, 1621 Superior Lincoln, NE, 68521. From the St. Luke's church history 2nd paragraph: "On March 19, 1891, Methodists felt it was time they had a church of their own as they had been meeting in homes. A religious Society was formed for the purpose of providing North Lincoln with a Methodist Church to be called Union Place M.E. Church. It was to be built at 7th and Irving. Mrs. L.A. Peters made a $500 contribution on condition the church would be called **"The Lucy Peters Memorial M.E. Church."** This condition was met and agreed upon. However, from the beginning it was called "Lincoln Heights" on the Conference minutes to designate its location. The Pastor of this church points out that Lucy Peters never attended this church nor was this church ever known as "The Lucy Peters Memorial M.E. Church."

Nellie Fontaine Memorial UMC, Box 164, Elwood, NE 68937 (now ? the Betrand UMC).

Mary A. Johnson Memorial UMC, Box 337 Ceresco, NE., 68017-0-337.

Hortense Ritter Memorial, Rt. 2, Box 34, Brock, NE., 68320 (? Elk Creek now).

Jane M. King UMC, Box 100, Orchard, NE., 68764 (? Orchard UMC now).

These are from the NE. Annual Conference, 2641 N. 49th, P.O. Box 4553, Lincoln, NE., 68504-0553

NEW HAMPSHIRE

Hannah Tenney Memorial UMC, 8 Pleasant St., Salem, NH., 03079-2907. When the First Methodist Church burned on March 16, 1917, the generosity of the sons of Hannah Tenney made possible the replacement church. They had been active members.

NEW JERSEY

Frances Childs UMC, of Collingswood, NJ.,412 White Horse Pike & Collings Avenue W., Collingswood, NJ., 08107. Phone: (856) 854-6890 Leo Park sent the information about this church. In 1899 a Sunday School started and grew into a Union Church and then waned. "If most churches begin with a Sunday School, it is true that it is the women...who keep a Church going." Mrs. John Peterson and Mrs. George Weilland made a personal canvass and received such a warm welcome by Mrs. Eldridge that they continued until the community had a church. On March 5, 1902 they organized as a Methodist Episcopal Church. Cornerstone laid June 20th, 1903.

The present church was from the idea of a new stone church that Frances Childs visualized and told her husband. After her death he had the stone church built and gave it to the congregation. On learning of Mr. Childs' plan the official board changed the church name to "Frances Childs Methodist Episcopal Church." It was dedicated on January 5, 1926 by Bishop Joseph F. Berry.

NEW YORK

Sarah Jane Johnson Memorial UMC is located on 308 Main Street in Johnson City, NY., 13790. Started in a shoe factory in 1890, it had been chartered in 1889. The trustees had two Johnsons, C. Fred and George. By 1905 they enlarged the church and bought a pipe organ. With a large generous donation by George F. Johnson, the cornerstone to the present Sarah Jane Johnson Church was laid in 1926 to honor his mother, a woman of beautiful Christian character.

Harkness UMC, named after Georgia Harkness, located 54 Spring St., Keeseville, NY., 12944. Dr. Georgia Harkness, Christian teacher, preacher, writer and poet. Professor of Applied Theology the Pacific School of Religion, Berkeley, CA., and a Methodist delegate to Faith and Order Conference of the World Council of Churches at Lund, Sweden. Look in your hymnal for her name.

NORTH CAROLINA

Info from Mr. Joyner 8809 Millers Bend, Bahama, NC., 27503-9611.

Saint Frances Church in the Elizabeth City District was named for a woman in the congregation many years ago. Rev. Jesse C. Styanton Jr. 4102 Neal Road., Durham, NC 27705.

It was built in 1848, complete with a slave gallery and a pump organ. Saint Frances Church was closed a few years ago, but the building is now a multi-cultural congregation called *"All God's Children UMC."* Rev. Laura G. Early, 1116 Hexlena Road, Ailander, 27805-9424.

Anna Jarvis in Yadkin County, NC. is a closed church previously in the Central Jurisdiction. The tradition for the name is unknown. In town of Yadkinville?

Mariah Chapel in Caldwell County, NC. was named after Martha Maria Ernest, who gave the land for the church in 1875. Maria or Mariah – it is the same woman. P.O. Box 584, Lenoir, NC 28645.

Bess Hoey Memorial UMC in Cleveland County, NC. was named after the wife of Clyde R. Hoey, a governor of North Carolina. Known as the Bess Chapel Memorial UMC. 2741 Hwy 274, Cherryville 28021.

Lousia Chapel in Haywood County, NC., is one of the oldest churches in the area. It grew out of Shook's Campground and was named after the granddaughter of Jacob Shook, who gave the land for the church. P.O. Box 85, Lake Junaluska, NC., 28745

Celia Phelps UMC in Guiford County, NC., is a predominately African American church. Tradition says that the money for the church was given by Celia Phelps' employer in her honor. 822 Mystic Drive, Greensboro, NC., 27406.

Rose Chapel UMC, 813 Turnersburg Highway, Statesville, NC., 28625. It was organized by W.H. Aderhold, W.H.H. Summers, A.C. Mores, N.F. Blakwelder and J.J. Nicholson. Aderhold and his brother-in-law, W.H. Cloyd gave the land. The building was started in 1903. The church was named in honor of Rose Aderhold, daughter of W.H. Aderhold. Rose and a friend, Turley Hollard went from home to home collecting money to build the first church. In April 1904 young Miss Rose died. She had collected about five dollars. This death inspired the adults and soon the needed money was offered and the church built. Miss Rose Aderholt is buried in the church graveyard and the present day secretary sent a rubbing of the stone. Fire destroyed the structure in 1942. It was rebuilt in 1944.

NORTH DAKOTA – none

OHIO
Nellie Chapel UMC in Warsaw, OH., 43844. Nellie Darling for whom the town was named. She served as its mayor in 1900. She married U.S. Moore. It was Nellie's father J.P. that named the town and organized the Evangelical Church.

Thoburn United Methodist Church, 101 North Market, St. Clairsville, OH. This church was named after two people, a sister and brother, James and Isabella. James became a Bishop 1836-1922 and it was this dedicated brother who, after graduating from college, left for the mission-field in India. There he penned an off-handed letter asking Isabella if she would like to join him in teaching. She went and for the next 20 years she taught and her school became the Isabella Thoburn College. She was the first Methodist woman missionary sent out on her own to the mission-field and was sponsored by Women's Foreign Missionary Society. The UMC stands in tribute to those Thoburns.

Mary Reed at Crooked Tree. P.O. Box 22, Macksburg, OH., 45746. Mary was a missionary to the lepers.

OKLAHOMA
Mary Lee Clark, Oklahoma Indian Mission at 1100 Howard Drive, Del City, OK., 73115. Formerly old St. Mark's Methodist.

Orva Mathes Memorial Methodist Church, Hooker, OK. Orva Lucy Mathes, daughter of Rev. W.C. and Lucy Banks, born in Grosebeck, TX., Sept. 16, 1908. Married W.C. Mathes Sept. 27, 1927. Orva enjoyed but a small measure of physical strength. She was happy, cheerful, unselfish and young people caught from her the vision of a more glorious life. The new church in Hooker was dedicated in her memory by Rev. C.E. Nisbett after her death on Sept. 4, 1941. Now the church is called the Hooker United Methodist Church.

McKee Methodist Church, Oklahoma City, OK. The McKee Chapel was named after Valie McKee who was a member of St. Mark's Methodist church. Her husband donated the land and lumber for the Chapel. This church is made up of three smaller churches: St. Mark's, McKee and Billy Hooten Memorial Church (formerly the First Methodist Church).

Humphrey's UMC in Sperry, OK. It was the birthing efforts of Mrs. D.W. Humphreys, Rev. Brannon and Rev. Wiles holding revivals in a tent in August 1924 that the Methodist church became a reality. The church was renamed on May 17, 1956, to honor Mrs. D.W. Humphreys, the mother of Dr. Buel H. Humphreys, who did so much in its establishment and preservation. It was said her inspiration and visualization moved this church to a higher conception of the presence of Divine Power.

OREGON – none

PENNSYLVANIA
Anne Ashley UMC, 334 Twenty-Second St., Munhall, PA., 15120-2546. Phone: (412) 462-3134.

The Jenny Lind UMC now part of the Hope UMC. 1907 Soles St., McKeesport, PA., 15132. Phone: (412) 673-5792.

Albright-Bethune UMC, W. Beaver and S. Burrowes St., State College, PA., 16804. Named after Jacob Albright and Mary McLeod Bethune. Mary was born on a small farm near Sumter, NC on July 10, 1875. She lived until 1955. Her mother said of her fifteenth of seventeen children, "Mary has a rising soul. She will either go far or break her heart." She was in luck when a Presbyterian missionary opened a school for black children. Mary walked the five miles each day. Attended Scotia Seminary in N.C. and Moody Institute in Chicago. She started the Daytona Educational and Industrial Training School in 1904. In 1922 it became a United Methodist related school known as the Bethune-Cookman College. In 1935 Roosevelt appointed her Negro Affairs Director in his National Youth Administration. Eleanor sent Franklin's cane to Mary with these words attached, "In inspiration not only to the people of your race, but to the world at large."

Mary C. Sellers Memorial UMC. Church in Upper Darby, PA. The cornerstone was laid on Sunday, September 11, 1921. On November 13, 1921 at the first service the three Sellers sisters were present – Mary, Sarah and Annabelle. Later the name was changed to Mary C. Sellers Methodist Episcopal Church.

Mary S. Brown UMC, 3424 Beechwood Blvd.,. Pittsburgh, PA., 15217. Phone: (412) 421-4431.

Crever Memorial UMC, King St., c/o RD 1, Box 424D, Alexandria, PA., 16611. The church was built as a memorial to Susan Caroline Follansbee Crever, wife of Rev. Dr. Benjamin H. Crever. He was the chief financial supporter and former pastor.

Hick's Memorial UMC, 1201 3rd Ave., Duncansville, PA., 16635. The building was proposed by Captain Alfred Hicks of Pittsburgh and named by him as a memorial to his parents – Philemon Nelson Hicks and Cecilia Morgan Hicks.

Jaggard Memorial UMC 4126 Broad Av., Altoona, PA., 16601. Mrs. C.E. Pugh gave the lots for the church at half price if the structure be named the "Mrs. Annie Jaggard Memorial Chapel" for her mother.

Mardorf UMC. Juniata Gap Road, RD 4, Box 204, Altoona, PA., 16601. When Mr. and Mrs. Plack gave the present church property, they asked that the official church name be that of Mr. Plack's grandmother – whose maiden name was Mardorf.

Saint Mary's UMC, 35 Mt. Rock Road, Newville, PA., 17421. The origin of the name is uncertain, but it is likely that the choice was made with a saintly woman named Mary from the local community in mind and not solely in honor of the earthly mother of Jesus.

Sumerville UMC, 203 Second St., P.O. Box 190, Sumerville, PA., 17093. The building was completed in 1910 with the official name of "Leah S. Robins Memorial Methodist Episcopal Church" and was named by the churches benefactor the Rev. Silas Comfort Swallow for his mother-in-law – Leah Shindle Robins.

Ellen Chapel EUB Ferguson Valley Rd., Lewistown, PA., 17044. This was a Methodist congregation until 2001. The church was named after the wife of the builder of the original structure, F.G. Franciscus. This congregation left the Ellen Chapel and joined EUB. They erected a new building.

Emmanuel UMC 22 Salt Rd., Enola, PA., 17025-2017. This congregation is the union of Methodists and EUBs and they erected a new building. The former Methodist building was the "Electa Dilley Memorial Methodist Episcopal Church" after the lady who contributed the first hundred dollars.

RHODE ISLAND – none

SOUTH CAROLINA
Emma Gray Memorial UMC, Woodruff, Spartanburg County, SC., 29388. Emma Swink Gray (1858-1909) inspired others, prayed, served, entertained ministers, prepared communion and was an ever-present member of the church's activities. Construction started in 1916. It was said of her "Her voice is silent, but the impress of her life will ever be felt."

Virginia Wingard UMC, 1500 Broad River Rd., Columbia, Richland County, SC., 29210. Virginia Ann (O'Brien) Wingard born on October 10, 1878 in Pelion, SC. Her father was a Professor at Crossroads Academy.

When Mrs. Wingard lost her husband ('38) and her daughter ('48) she became grief-stricken. This is what she wrote in the Chapel at Columbia Hospital, "In this chapel on this holy ground, I prayed and found strength to bear to see my daughter, my only child go home to be face-to-face with the Lord. He is Love and Mercy. V.W."

She became known as an Ambassador of Goodwill in her going from bedside to bedside. Her wonderful spirit led her to visit the sick and at the end of the many visits she slipped in a bed exhausted and fell asleep to meet her Saviour on Jan. 26, 1953.

Ann Hope UMC, 2312 E. Ashton St., Seneca, Oconee, SC., 29678.

SOUTH DAKOTA
Cornelia Naylor Memorial Methodist Episcopal Church, Fairmount, SD. The church was named after the daughter of a woman (from some family out east nobody in Fairmount knew) who had donated a significant amount of money ($1000) to the church (from a remembrance of a member.)

Kittie Edwards Memorial Methodist Episcopal at Cresbard, SD. Kittie Bromaghim was born to Mahlon and Catherine Bromaghim near Ogdensburg, St. Lawrence, New York on Feb. 16, 1876. At ten she came to Redfield, South Dakota. On Feb. 12, 189? married Noah Edwards Jr. Kittie taught school. She was always ready to help others. Her husband was not listed among the mourners at her funeral on Feb. 12, 1905. He was killed, walked out on her or what? Perhaps that is a sorrow she silently bore while she did her Christian help for others. Kittie

Edwards was the deceased sister of the Rev. Frank
Bromghin who organized the church in 1907. Building
was dedicated December 29, 1907. Upon the building of a
new church in 1971, the name was changed to Cresbard
UMC.

TENNESSEE
Nancy Webb Kelly UMC on South 8th St., Nashville,
Davidson County, TN. Shirley Majors-Jones is the pastor.
Phone (615) 227-1953. E-mail: <u>cody@aol.com</u>

Annie Morrison Smith Memorial UMC in downtown
Nashville, TN. was closed with the building of a freeway.
The Underwoods of this congregation were charter
member of Nancy Webb Kelly UMC.

Mary Chaffin Memorial is located 715 Lake Street in
Labanon, Wilson County, TN., 37087. Named after a
Pastor who became blind but continued to serve her
congregation. She was aided by chauffeur. Sean V. Cook
Sr. is the pastor and lives at 111 Joiner Av., Nashville,
TN., 37210.

Ruth Ensor UMC in Dayon City, TN. Rehea county,
(Old Hickory). Ernest Lamely is pastor and lives at 114
Longboat Ct., Gallain, TN., 37066.

Keith Memorial UMC, Athens TN. In 1904 land was
given by Mrs. A.H. Keith for the first parsonage. In the
1939 church reunion of South and North the church was
renamed the Keith Memorial Methodist Church.
Boose Memorial UMC, 805 Merriman St., Dyersburg,
TN., 38024-3421. Mrs. Boose was the first woman to be

licensed to preach in the Central Tennessee Conference in 1939. She pastors five churches: Bednton, Decatur and Henderson Counties and one in Parson. Married in 1939, she and Mr. C.E. worked in missions under Dr. Lud Estes. Mrs. Boose died April 19, 1973. Church closed in 1996.

TEXAS
Moody Memorial UMC 2803 53rd St.,, Galvaston, TX., 77551-5999. Named after Liblie Sharon Moody.

Tapp Memorial UMC, New Boston, TX., 75570-0035. The church was dedicated May 23, 1939 by Bishop A. Frank Smith. This church is named for Miss Jennie Tapp who gave $23,000 to New Boston church and also to a Methodist church in Mauc, Texas; and gifts to Lon Morris College and Southern University and the Methodist Home.

UTAH – none

VERMONT
Rachel E. Harlow UMC was dedicated February 4, 1896 in Windsor, Windsor County, VT. Church records show that three years earlier Mrs. Harlow had left $10,000 in her will for the purpose of buying the land and erecting a church in Windsor. Located on 165 Main St., Windsor, VT., 05089-0756. Pastor Rev. Carter Adrance.

VIRGINIA
Susanna Wesley UMC, 3900 George Washington Highway, Ordinary, VA., 23131. This church took the name of John and Charles Wesley's mother Susanna in 1988. They were a mission of the Rappahannock District

and the "Revealing Christ" campaign of the Virginia
Annual Conference. They now have 283 members and
growing. P.O. Box 427. Rev. Walton C. Forestall 2nd.

Madam Russell Memorial UMC, P.O. Box JJ, 207 West
Main St., Saltville, VA., 24370

Elizabeth Henry Campbell Russell, a sister to the well-
known Patrick Henry, married Col. William Campbell in
Hanover County in 1776. After the battle of "King's
Mountain" he became a general. He died in 1781 at the
home of his wife's step-brother awaiting the surrender of
Yorktown. In 1782 Elizabeth married General William
Russell. The Russells attended the First Methodist
Conference in May 1788. Along with Bishop Asbury,
Madam Russell hosted many pioneer itinerant Methodist
Ministers. In Saltville, in 1824, a Methodist church,
Elizabeth Church, was dedicated in her name.

In 1898 a new church was begun just a few feet from
the Russell home. That church stands today as a
monument to Mrs. Russell, the region's earliest religious
leader in the Holston Territory of Southwest Virginia and
Northeast Tennessee. A registered UM Historical Site.

Elizabeth Chapel, 5522 Sugar Grove Hwy, Sugar
Grove VA., 24375 – It is reported that the sons of widow
Elizabeth Rodgers were among the church members who
pitched in to clear the land, saw the timber and erect the
new building. When it was dedicated, it was renamed the
Elizabeth Chapel in honor of Elizabeth Rodgers.

WASHINGTON
Mary Emma Tibbetts UMC at 3421 41 SW, Seattle,
King County, WA., 98116-3421. In 1907 Mrs. Tibbets

willed three lots on 41st Ave. Southwest to this church. She was born May 27, 1838 and lived in Seattle and was a member of Grace Methodist in Seattle.

Fowler UMC, North 3928 Howard St., Spokane, WA., Spokane County, 99205. The widow had some money, unusual for a preacher's wife. She had missions as her goal for those living in Philadelphia the west was a mission field. Small amounts then larger were sent to the Home Mission project. A great controversy over the name, but her interest and generosity won out and the church was built in 1906.

WEST VIRGINIA

Elizabeth Memorial UMC, Pastor Dr. Frank Shomo. 108 Oakwood Dr., Charleston, WV., 25314. Was organized in 1896 in a storeroom under the Odd Fellows Hall by Rev. B.A. Winn. Elizabeth Memorial moved to Oakwood in 1977. The first church, built in 1902, was located at 804 Myrtle Road. That building is now a Presbyterian Church. That site was donated by the South Charleston Land Improvement Co. "Uncle Bob" R.S. Carr was largely responsible for that gift. In appreciation of his many gifts and influence the church was named in memory of his wife's mother, Mrs. Elizabeth Wilson.

Florence Memorial UMC, Dickson, WV. – It was October 7, 1951 when member a Mt. Vernon Methodist church and Martha Ann Methodist Church witnessed the merger to the Florence Memorial UMC. The new church was named in honor of Florence Bing McGinnis, the mother of Addie Earp, their organist.

Martha Ann Methodist, merged with the Florence Memorial UMC at Dickson, WV.

Elizabeth Memorial UMC in Braxton United Methodist Charge in Sutton-Gassaway, WV. The church was named after two women – Elizabeth Gerwig and Elizabeth Perrine, wives of two men who were probably the most influential in building the church in 1903. The church was organized in 1895.

Elizabeth UMC, Pastor David Stackpole. Box 549, Elizabeth, WV., 26143. This may be named after the town?

Bethany UMC, Pastor Cynthia Eakle, P.O. Box 6, Palisine, WV., 26160.

Delilah UMC, Oceana, WV. The churchsite was donated by Bert Cook, a fifth-generation descendant of John and Nellie. The church is located on a part of the original homestead of John Cook (1799). Their graves are in the churchyard. Bert Cook sponsored and promoted the organizing of this church and he was given the honor of naming this house of worship. He chose the name of his mother who had died when he was five.

Mount Sarah Methodist in the Elana Charge, WV. When the Methodist Society was founded in the Sinclair Community they used a schoolhouse for their meetings. In 1889 Sarah Sinclair died and was buried next to the schoolhouse. The widower, Mr. Hector Sinclair gave the land for the building next to the schoolhouse. The church was built by local volunteers. Charles Felton made the

pews. Church was dedicated in 1907 and was served by
the Methodist of Elana.

Mariah Chapel in Clemtown, WV. In 1876 the church
was built and was named Mariah Chapel in memory of
one of God's noble women, the first to be laid to rest in its
cemetery.

Miller Memorial UMC, Miller Av., Hinton, WV. The
class was organized in 1915. The church building
dedicated on July 30, 1944. It was named in memory of
William Erskin and Sarah Barbar Miller who were the
parents of the men who built the building.

Rebecca, Sophia and Leronma are from a letter of
Carl G. Wolfe – "...I regret to tell you that while they were
named after women, they were the wives and mothers of
coal owners and operators. ...one more example –
Mabscott was named after Mabel Scott."

Gertrude Chapel, WV. Jessie Gertrude Talbot Osburn
(1880-1966) wife of Van Buren Osburn. She donated the
land for the church. Info from Amy W. Tenney – RR 9,
Box 315, Buckannon, WV., 26201-8509.
E-mail: <u>tenney@neumedia.net</u>

WISCONSIN
Mary Cain Church, WI. In 1899 the young people of
the United Brethren church in Bloomer, Wisconsin
conceived the idea of having a church named after Mrs.
Mary Cain, a martyred missionary who was slain in
Africa. Isaac and Mary served at Rotifunk, Sierra Leone.
They were massacred on May 3, 1898. Eleven members
signed the charter in 1901. The church building was

completed in 1902. 1946 Evangelical Association and United Brethren in Christ joined to form the Evangelical United Brethren Church. 1968 Methodist Episcopal merged with Evangelical United Brethren to form the UMC at 1700 South Main St., Bloomer, WI., 54724. Phone (715) 568-1971. Pastor Mark W. Geisthardt.

WYOMING

Berta A. Penney Memorial in Kemmerer, WY. This church was founded by Bishop Edward W. Pupa, and he said "...named after the wife of J.C. Penney." WY. is the state where J.C. started his partnership stores. In 1910, 8 years after his first store, he and his wife planned a trip to Europe, a delayed honeymoon. Berta had a tonsillectomy then caught a cold and soon died in Kemmerer. J.C. must have made a substantial contribution to the local church.

– Index –

– A –

– B –

Frank Bell, Unitarian minister, Boothbay, Jan 1906
Burton, barber in Hartland, April 1907
Buck family, Hartland, May 1907
Dr. Baker, Hartland, Aug. 1907
Mrs. Baker, Hartland book club, Oct. 1907
Mr. Blanchard, Hartland druggist, Aug. 1907
Mrs. Brown, Hartland Unitarians, Oct. 1907
Mary Brown, member Caribou UMC, July 1910
Elmer Brayson, Aroostook county sheriff, Jan. 1911
Ray Brown, member Caribou MEC, June 1911
Rev. Blair, Caribou's Unitarian minister, Sept. 1911
Berce, buyer of old Caribou's MEC building, Dec. 1911
Bishops William Bart, Rockland conference, April 1912
George V. Brown, Sunday School leader, Sept. 1912
Mrs. Bouchard, Caribou's Ladies Relief Corps, June 1913
Albert Belyea, Dec. 1913
Bishops Joseph Berry, at Dover Conference, April 1915
Rev. Bishop, a local Caribou minister, June 1918
Emme & Frank Barry, Port Elgin, April 1914
Carl Berg, Port Elgin, April 1915
William Boyce, Port Elgin, May 1915
Roy Bradley, Port Elgin, May 1915
Roy Bradley, Port Elgin, May 1915
Carl Berg, Port Elgin, March 1916
Alvie Baker, Port Elgin, June 1917
John Berry, Port Elgin, June 1917

– C –

Fred Clark, Port Elgin, June 1889
Mrs. Clark, piano teacher and choir leade,r Aug. 1892
Hazen Copp, Port Elgin, May 1889
Tammy Copp, fellow student of Bessie, Aug. 1891
William Chapman, fellow student of Bessie, Aug. 1891
Rev. Chapman, methodist minister, Aug. 1892
G. Cleveland, running for President, Oct. 1892
Helen Chamberlain-Epworth, Hyde Park, Dec. 1897
Rev. George L. Collyer, pastor at Hyde Park, Feb. 1897
D.B. Conant, church member, Cushing, June 1899

"Candy" "The Cat", Dec. 1899
Mr. Champney, druggist, Rockport, July 1900
Dr. Carter, physician, Boothbay, June 1903
Rev. H.L. Calkins, Hartland Baptist minister, May 1907
Willa Cather, author, Oct. 1907
Mary Campbell, member Caribou MEC, Jan. 1911
Bishop Earl Cranston, Old Town Conference, April 1911
Andrew Carnegie, a philanthropist, June 1911
Dr. Cary, Caribou physician and philanthropist, Sept. 1912
Harold Chadwick, Houlton florist, Nov. 1913
Bertha and Ernest Cobb, authors, Oct. 1914
Chenny, a local Caribou minister, June 1918
Norton Copp, Port Elgin, Dec. 1914
Albert Carter, Port Elgin, May 1915

– D –

Mr. Dakin, band leader, Aug. 1892
James Dobson, uncle, Port Elgin, July 1896
Joe Dobson, uncle
George Dotty, Pres. Epworth League, Hyde Park, March 1901
John Doyle, fellow student, Port Elgin, May 1901
Dickins, author, Dec. 1901
Mona Davis, member Caribou MEC, June 1911
Jane Dupont, member Caribou MEC, June 1911
Percy Dow, lay preacher, Washburn Methodist, Dec. 1911
Rev. W.F. Davis DD of Houlton at Caribou MEC, Nov. 1913
Rev. G.F. Durgin, East Maine Conf. Sem., Nov. 1913
Mona Davis, Caribou, member of MEC, June 1911
Warren Dobson, Port Elgin, March 1916
Ray Dugay, Port Elgin, Sept. 1917

– E –

Rev. William Edmund, pastor Caribou MEC, June 1910
H.W. Ebbett, Caribou Church building, Jan. 1911
Gretchen Ebbett, daughter, Caribou MEC, Jan. 1911
Mrs. Gretchen Ebbett, mother, Caribou MEC, Jan. 1911
Ray Ebbett, member Caribou MEC, June 1911
Rev. Gilbert Edgett, Methodist Pastor, Dec. 1914

Mrs. Harriet Eaton, Livermore Falls, Oct. 1915
Erving, Caribou, Dec. 1911

– F –

Jack and Dolly Freeze, Dec. 1890
John Freeland, member of church at Amherst, Jan. 1894
A.S. Fales, Cushing, freight, May 1899
Folger, Editor of Rockland newspaper, Dec. 1901
Mr. Fisher, dry goods store, Boothbay, June 1903
Mrs. Amos Fletcher Sr., Jan. 1911
Rev. Ferguson, Caribou's Baptist minister, Sept. 1911
Farrel, co-buyer of old MEC building, Dec. 1911
John Flood, Bucksport methodist, April 1913
Mrs. Olley Fair, Sept. 1914
Fillmores, Port Elgin, May 1915
Fred Fitzpatrick, Port Elgin, March 1916

– G –

James Gray, May 1889
John Gray, James father, Dec. 1890
Rachel Gray, James mother, Dec. 1890
Ora Samuel Gray, brother revivalist, Dec. 1890
Thomas Gray, Hyde Park, Ma., June 1897
Frederickl Griffith, student BU, June 1897
John Gould, author and farmer in Friendship, Oct. 1899
Gray, a member Caribou MEC, April 1902
Fred Greene, Boothbay, Jan. 1905
Bishop Goodspell, April, 1905
Evangelist Gale, Oct. 1908
Alice Griffin, member Caribou MEC, July 1910
W.A. Gray, member Caribou MEC, Jan. 1911
Livi Gray, horse dealer, Caribou, Oct. 1911
Ezekiel Gonier, member Caribou's MEC, Oct. 1911
A.J. Goud, former owner MEC parsonage, Dec. 1911
Rev. Carl Garland, District Superintendent, April 1916
Isac Gray, Port Elgin, Dec. 1914
Jim Goodwin, Port Elgin, May 1915
James & Monsel Goodwin, Port Elgin, March 1915

Alonzo Goodwin, Port Elgin, Jan. 1917
Willis & Guy, Sept. 1917

– H –

Lorenza Howard, Port Elgin, June 1889
Dr. Harrison, Principal at the Acedemy, Dec. 1890
Harrison, running for President, Oct. 1892
Haskels Shoe Shop, Hyde Park, MA., Sept. 1897
Mrs. Harthorn, church lady at Cushing, May 1899
Billy Hyde, Rockport, Jan. 1901
F.E. Hale, a member Caribou MEC, Dec. 1911
Hight, a member of Caribou MEC, Dec. 1911
Robert and Stella Hogdons, friends, Boothbay, Aug. 1903
Fred Harris, Boothbay, Aug. 1903
Rev. Harry Holt, Minister, April 1908
Jane Hill, student at Hartland, Sept. 1907
Mrs. Hoyt, Hartland Book Club, Oct. 1907
Mrs. Haley, Hartland Book Club Oct. 1907
Bishop John Hamilton, Houlton, April 1908
Evangelist Hatch, Oct. 1907
Pearl Higgins, Sept. 1909
Father Joseph Hogan, RC priest at Caribou, May 1910
Sarah Harmon, member Caribou MEC, July 1910
F.E. Hale, member of Caribou MEC, April 1902
Rev. Harry Holt, Minister, April 1904
Rev. John Howes, Methodist local pastor, May 1911
Havey's, a drugstore in Caribou, June 1911
Mrs. Hussey, Caribou, March 1912
Rev. Harry Adams Hersey, Caribou Union Church, Nov. 1912
Bishop Theodore Henderson, at Bucksport, April 1913
Bishop John Hamilton, dedication of MEC, Nov. 1914
Mr. and Mrs. Charles Harrington of Rockland, May 1915
Mrs. and Mrs. Herbert Hitchings, Caribou MEC, June 1918
David Hitchings, son of Herbert, June 1918
Robert Hebert, Port Elgin, May 1915
Thorne Hayward, Port Elgin, Feb. 1916

– I –

Mrs. Grace Linn, Hartland Church, May 1907
Charles Lovejoy, Hartland carpenter, July 1907
Hellen Linn, grand-daughter of Grace, Hartland, Aug. 1907
Archibald Linn, husband of Grace, Aug. 1907
Rev. J.J. Lowe, evangelist, Jan. 1911
John B. Lyon, member Caribou MEC (occ Lyons), Jan. 1911
Longfellow, Maine poet, Feb. 1911
Dr. Little, Caribou physician, June 1911
Rev. Albert Luce, Methodist ministe,r April 1914
Rev. Isaac Lidstone, minister at Caribou, April 1915
Roy Lamb, Port Elgin, May 1915
Legers, Port Elgin, May 1915
Bishops Frederick Leete, April 1917
Georgia Lyons, daughter of James, June 1918

– M –

Milton's store, Port Elgin, June 1889
Elda Murray, Port Elgin, June 1889
William MacLeod, Port Elgin, June 1889
Albert Mack, music teacher at the Academy, Dec. 1890
Charles Murray, fellow student of Bessie, Aug. 1891
Rev. McKay, methodist minister, Aug. 1892
Susannah Monro, Bessie's aunt, Aug. 1892
MacDonald, Premier of Canada, Oct. 1892
McKennas, family at Hyde Park, MA, Aug. 1897
Dr. K. McHight, physician, Hyde Park, MA., Sept. 1897
Leo and Annie McPhee, family at Hyde Park, MA., Sept. 1897
William McKinley, President, Sept. May 1897
Dr. George Morris, Professor at BU, May 1899
Albion Morse, church member, Cushing, Aug. 1899
Frank McNuttly, Train accident in Boston, July 1899
Alex McGrover, minister, Cushing, Aug. 1899
William Morse, Baptist pastor, Cushing, Aug. 1899
Fred McClellan, Cushing, Nov. 1899
Alex McGrover, Advent pastor and town clerk, Aug. 1899
Charles Morse, MEC pastor and friend, April 1900
Mr. Mather, Rockport fisherman, June 1901
Mitchell, Adventist minister, Rockport, July 1901
June and Jane McFarlane, Boothbay, Dec. 1905

Bishop David Moore, Vinalhaven, April 1906
Ralph Murray, Saint John, N.B., May 1907
Dr. Moulton, Hartland, Aug. 1909
Mrs. Moulton, Hartland Book Club, Aug. 1907
Mr. Miller, Hartland select man, Aug. 1907
Mrs. Miller, Hartland Bookstore, Oct. 1907
Rev. Charles McEthiney, Caribou pastor '90-93, June 1911
Rev. Albert E. Morris, District Superintendent, Nov. 1913
Rev. Henry Marr, minister, Mapleton, April 1915
Mr. and Mrs. Caleb Moffit, Rockland, May 1915
John Munroe, Port Elgin, Dec. 1915
Mrs. McNaught, nurse helper for Bessie, May 1918
Minor, a local Caribou minister, June 1918
Percy Murray, Dec. 1914
George & James Manship, Port Elgin, April 1915
Mayo & Rose, April 1916
Frank McKay, Port Elgin, Jan. 1917
Hugh, Carl & Sedley Moore, Port Elgin, July 1917
Clarence Mitton, Port Elgin, Jan. 1918

– N –
Alonzo Nickerson, Boothbay
J.S. Norton, Hartland, May 1907
Howard Nichols, barn in Limestone, Nov. 1912
Olaf Nylander, scientist, Nylander Museum, Nov. 1914
Joseph Nedeau, serviceman, died of flu, Aug. 1918

– O –
Frank Osgood, BU student, May 1898
Avery Oulton, married Bessie's siter, Nov. 1901
Floyd Oulton, Port Elgin, March 1916

– P –
Joe Puffer, BU student from Harrington, ME., March 1898
Ernest Plummer, fellow student, Port Elgin, April 1901
Rev. Frank T. Pomeroy, pastor, Hyde Park, July 1897
Fred Palladino, BU student, May 1898
Don Piper, BU student, May 1898

Will Patten, BU student, May 1898
John Pinkerton, MEC pastor, and friend, April 1900
Mr. Palmer, Rockport fisherman, June 1901
F.M. Polards, Caribou Church building committee, April 1902
Mrs. Polards, Jan. 1911
Corydon Powers, a member of Caribou MEC, April 1902
Elmer & Delbert Powers, Corydon's twin sons, June 1911
Bertha Leola Powers, July, 1910
Gov. Powers, Nov. 1913
Olaf Pierson, married Corydon's daughter, June 1911
Robert Perry, goes to North Pole, Nov. 1909
F.M. Poland, member Caribou MEC, Jan. 1911
Mrs. Mita Poland, member Caribou MEC, June 1918
Mr. F.M. Poland, member Caribou MEC, May 1910
Austin Poland, grandson of Ansel G. Taylor, June 1918
E.E. Powers, Caribou automobile sales, May 1911
Page, Dec. 1911
P.J. Powers, Caribou, Sept. 1912
Ralph Pitcher, Caribou farmer, Nov. 1912
Governor Powers, Maine Governor, June 1911
Rev. Charles Plumber, methodist minister, April 1914
Rev. George Pratt, Rockland, Oct. 1915
Perly Palmer, serviceman – killed, Oct. 1918
George Parks, Port Elgin, Jan. 1917
Joseph Prescott, Port Elgin, Jan. 1917
Henry Pratt, July 1918

– Q –

Bishop William Qualey, Calais conference, April 1910

– R –

Sillker Raworth, Port Elgin, N.B. Canada, March 1889
Millicent (Dobson) Raworth, March 1889
Courtney Raworth, son, March 1889
Bessie Raworth, daughter, March 1889
Ernest Raworth, son, March 1889
Reta Raworth, daughter, March 1889
Eva Robinson, fellow student of Bessie Aug. 1891

Dr. Rallis, physician, Amherst, Nova Scotia, Sept. 1895
Jacob Raworth, uncle, Port Elgin, Dec. 1895
William and Ruth Raworth, Port Elgin, July 1896
Rupert Raworth, son of Courtney, Feb. 1897
Sarah, Aunt of Bessie, Jan. 1897
Vaughn Raworth, son of Courtney, April, 1899
Victor Raworth, son of Ernest
Calvin Raworth, Port Elgin, Jan. 1901
Roy Raworth, son of Courtney, also called Ray, April 1901
Bessie Raworth, daughter of Courney, May 1905
Everret Raworth, son of Courtney, Aug. 1914
Gordon Ross, student BU, June 1897
Henry Routley, tailor, Hyde Park, MA., July 1897
Theodore Roosevelt, US Navy, Sept. 1897
Rev. Ramsdell, Caribou's Baptist minister, Nov. 1912
Amos Riley, Port Elgin, March 1916
Will Riley, Port Elgin, March 1916

– S –

James Smith, student at the Academy, Dec. 1890
Asa Strong, student at the Academy, Dec. 1890
Cilia Simpson, fellow student of Bessie, Aug. 1891
Cora Silliker, cousin of Bessie, Aug. 1891
George Stocking, trustee, Hyde Park MEC., MA., Nov. 1897
Anna Howard Shaw, well-known at BU Theology School 1899
Anna Shaw, Famous Methodist woman, May 1899
Captain J.A. Simmons, Cushing, Oct. 1899
Charles Smith, pastor MEC, friend, March 1900
Ralph Spear, church member, Rockport, May 1900
Will Stow, Universalist minister, Rockport, Sept. 1900
Mr. & Mrs. Stitham, a member of Caribou MEC, April 1902
Scott, a member of Caribou MEC, April 1902
Joe Skidgel, farmer, Boothbay, June 1903
James Swift, student from Bangor seminary, June 1904
Shaw, Forest company, June 1905
Stofords, Dec. 1905
Oscar Strauss, author, Oct. 1907
Mrs. Smith, Hartland Book Club, Oc. 1907

Mrs. Floyd Sweet and son James, June 1910
Upton Sinclair, author, Nov. 1907
Sarah Smith, member Caribou UMC, July 1910
Viola Sousis, member Caribou UMC, June, 1910
Mr. L.G. Smith, member Caribou MEC., Jan. 1911
Mr. S.M. Straight, member Cariobu MEC, Jan. 1911
A.W. Spaulding, Hardware owner, Cariobu, June 1911
Atwood William Spaulding, wedding, June 1911
Bertha Spaulding, A.D.' daughter, June 1911
Dr. Edgar W. Sincock, member of Caribou MEC., Oct. 1911
O.D. Smith, Caribou Church building, Dec. 1911
Jacob Smith, Caribou, Dec. 1911
Bessie Smith, Jacob's daughter, Dec. 1911
Floyd Smith, husband of Bessie Smith, Dec. 1911
Andrew Sockalexis, Maine Indian, Aug. 1912
Mary Shaw, Sept. 1912
Dr. Sincock, May 1913
Rev. George Stott, pastor at Presque Isle, May 1914
Mrs. Sleeper, Caribou, wife of store owner, May 1915
Mrs. and Mrs. Snow, Rockland, May 1915
Max Simpson, member of Craibou's MEC, June 1918
Frank Simpson, member of Caribou's MEC, June 1918
Donald Sutherland, Caribou – killed in war, June 1918
George Smith, Port Elgin, April 1915
Ivy Scott, Port Elgin, Jan. 1917

– T –

Blance Turner, Port Elgin, May 1889
Botsfords Turner, Port Elgin, May 1889
Rev. Teed, Port Elgin, June 1889
Sam Turner, Port Elgin, fellow student, Aug. 1891
John Terry, trustee, Hyde Park MEC., MA., Nov. 1897
Mark Twian, author, March 1899
Rev. W.A. Thompson, minister in Port Elgin, Sept. 1903
Rev. David Tribou, secretary of conference, March 1908
Celia & Sadie Turner, Caribou MEC., March 1912
Dr. Trustee, physician, Caribou, March, 1911
Todd, President of B & A Railroad, Nov. 1913

Dr. Tuell, June 1911
Charles Turner, Dec. 1914

– V –

John Vincent, ME., Bishop at Pittsfield, April 1904
Van Kiltons, Bar Harbor, April 1907
Mr. C.E. Varnum Caribou Church building, Jan. 1911
Vinals, Caribou girls, June 1911.

– W –

Jim Wheatly, student at the Academy, Dec. 1890
Weaver, US politician, Aug. 1892
Whites, family at Hyde Park, MA., Aug. 1897
Rev. Whitaker, pastor, Hyde Park, MEC. MA., Nov. 1897
Dr. William Warren, President school of Theology, May 1899
Rev. A.F. Wenchenback, Pastor of MEC., May 1899
Mrs. and Mrs. Wotton, shipbuilders, Cushing, July 1899
Chalres Wesley, Hymn writer, Jan. 1900
John Wesley, founder of Methodism, Jan. 1900
Dr. Weideman, physician, Rockport, Aug. 1900
Walker, minister for Episcopal, Rockport, July 1901
Bishop Henry Warren, Bar Harbor, April 1907
Fred Wyman, Hartland grocer, May 1907
Mr. Webber, Hartland selectman, Aug. 1907
James Watson at Houlton Conference, April 1908
Bishop Luther Wilson, Bucksport Conference, March 1909
Sarah Washburn, member, Caribou UMC, June 1910
Rev. James Withee, Methodist, local pastor, May 1911
Bud Wood, Caribou's storyteller, Nov. 1911
Woodrow Wilson, President, Aug. 1912
Avis Washburn, at Powers wedding, Caribou, Nov. 1913
Al and Will Walton, Port Elgin, May 1915

Bessie Raworth Gray

These portraits of
Bessie and James Gray
hang in the narthex of
the Bessie Gray
Memorial United
Methodist Church on
the corner of Sweden
and Prospect Streets in
Caribou, Aroostook
County, state of Maine,
U.S.A.

James Gray

About the Author

Phil Turner was born on a dairy and potato farm in Mapleton, Maine in the early 1920's. After high school, he left for the University of Maine – because he could no longer stand the cows! After graduating from the University of Massachusetts with a Masters degree, he earned a Ph.D. in Soil Science and Business Administration at Michigan State University.

Philip and Jean

Photo by
Voscar The Maine Photographer

His work experience was eclectic. After leaving DuPont in 1960, he returned to The County.

Turner's I AM General Eaton! was nominated for the William Young Boyd Military Novel Award. He received the Golden Book Award from the Maine Round Table Writers for the best regional historical novel.

– Bibliography –

East Maine Conference's reports of the Methodist Episcopal Church in yearbooks from 1899 to 1925 at the Bangor Theological Seminary.

Aroostook Republican newspapers at the Caribou Library. The Whitneck books.

Gray Memorial UMC – archives at the Caribou church and many other archivists in the U.S.A.

Boston University Library and archives of the United Methodist Church, Boston, MA.

The Library at Mount Allison University, Sackville, New Brunswick.

The Archives at the University of New Brunswick, Fredericton.

The Historical Society of Port Elgin, New Brunswick.

The Historical Society of Hyde Park, MA.

The Official United Methodist Church webserver: http://www.umc.org

The First Methodist
Worship Meeting House in Caribou
– 1887 –

The Methodist Church
Caribou, Maine